Raising

Girls

Who

Like

Themselves

Raising *Girls*

Who

Like

Themselves

KASEY EDWARDS

DR CHRISTOPHER SCANLON

PENGUIN LIFE

UK | USA | Canada | Ireland | Australia
India | New Zealand | South Africa | China

Penguin Life is part of the Penguin Random House group of companies whose
addresses can be found at global.penguinrandomhouse.com

First published by Penguin Life in 2021

Cover image by majivecka/Shutterstock.com
Cover design by Louisa Maggio © Penguin Random House Australia Pty Ltd
Typeset in 11/16 pt Berkeley by Midland Typesetters, Australia

Printed and bound in Australia by Griffin Press, an accredited
ISO AS/NZS 14001 Environmental Management Systems printer

A catalogue record for this
book is available from the
National Library of Australia

ISBN 978 1 76089 436 8

penguin.com.au

To parents

Contents

Foreword

Dear fellow parent,

Thank you for picking up our book. We' have daughters, too. Violet is ten and Ivy is a unicorn (also known as five). At this stage our girls are very different from each other. If they one day decide to go backpacking around Europe together, it wouldn't surprise us if Violet critiques the art inside the Louvre while Ivy scales the pyramid outside.

Like every generation before us, we want our children to have lives that are better than ours – more secure and filled with greater opportunities. We want them to be wealthier than us, and we're not just talking about material wealth. While a certain level of financial stability is important for a secure and independent life, we want our girls to be wealthier in spirit.

We want our daughters to be curious and independent and ambitious. We want them to make good choices, to have the resilience to bounce back from their 'it seemed like a good idea at the time' decisions, and to possess the strength to recover from plain bad luck. More than anything, we want them to have the courage to be real. We want them to understand themselves and to genuinely like who they are. If we were to boil down our goal as parents, it would be: we want to raise girls – and the women they become – who love themselves as much as we love them. Unconditionally.

If we can get this right then we figure everything else will follow. They will strive for excellence not because they're the hectored cubs of tiger mothers and fathers, but because they have faith in their ability to achieve it. They will range far beyond their comfort zones because they're adventurous and because failure is just a sign that they're still learning. They'll have the confidence to pick themselves up and try again. They will insist on healthy relationships because they will believe they deserve nothing less. They will nurture their physical and mental health because it's natural to care for what you love. They will be empathetic and open-minded because they will not be threatened by difference or need to tear other people down to feel better about themselves. They will be joyful and strong, knowing they are their own greatest friend and most capable ally.

'Yeah, good luck with that,' we hear you say. 'Do you plan on raising your kids in the middle of nowhere with no access to the internet, or the beauty, fashion and weight-loss industries, or school bullies, or patronising or sleazy adults?'

And you have a point.

The challenges facing this generation of girls as they attempt to develop and hold onto a healthy, happy and secure sense of self are daunting. We know as well as any parent that the odds are stacked against us. But we refuse to accept that the battle for our girls' well-being has already been fought and lost. There is too much at stake not to fight for their right to grow up whole and safe.

Through our writing, we have spent a decade calling out inequality and chipping away at our culture that dehumanises and devalues girls and women. But progress is slow so, when it comes to raising our own girls, we are focused on what we can control – what we can do right now. We cannot single-handedly kill off the cultural disease that is robbing so many of our girls of their potential, so instead we concentrate our attention on prevention and inoculation.

What we *can* do is think about our own childhoods, rethink parenting prejudices, pull apart our accepted cultural norms and stereotypes, talk to friends, make mistakes, re-evaluate (and then make yet more mistakes and re-evaluate again) and look at evidence to give our daughters the best chance possible in a world that too often encourages girls to make themselves small.

We are not claiming that ours is a foolproof parenting prescription. There is no single right way to raise a daughter. Families are different, children are different, and our capacity to parent the way we want to varies enormously from one day to the next. Some days it changes from hour to hour. As any parent knows, the gap between how we *think* we should raise kids and what we *actually* do takes on the proportions of the Grand Canyon when we are tired, stressed, busy, or just really need some time to ourselves.

And you know what? That's okay. Children don't need perfect parents. They just need good-enough parents.

Rather than writing an expert parenting manual that dictates a series of lovely-in-theory-but-never-going-to-happen guilt-inducing parenting rules, we have set out to share our risk-mitigation strategy for parenting our daughters. It's the perspective of both a mother and a father who face the same parenting challenges that you do right now. It's what we endeavour to do most of the time, within the constraints of life and our imperfect selves, to raise daughters who like themselves.

This book is for parents with girls who range from toddlers to tweens. It's about connecting the many dots of modern parenting advice on raising girls, helping you to develop an approach that fits with your values, works with your family dynamics – and, most of all, works for your daughters. We hope to give you some new insights and tools that will be helpful in raising your own girls – as well as a few laughs along the way, and a sense of solidarity and courage as we fight for our daughters' futures.

Kasey and Chris

Disclaimer

This book is based on our own experiences of raising two girls, watching children interact, many hours of conversation with other parents, and a decade of trawling through research about children, parenting, education and culture. It reflects our own perspectives – perspectives that are inevitably limited. Families come in all different forms: heterosexual parents, same-sex parents, separated and blended families, legal guardians and multi-generational families, all of which can be springs of love. Because we are the parents of girls, we have chosen to focus specifically on how to raise girls who like themselves. However, much of the research and our parenting strategies also apply to raising boys and non-binary children. For simplicity we have also referred to the carers of children as 'parents', 'mothers' and 'fathers'. We consider these to be roles that can be fulfilled by any number of people in a child's life, not limited by biology, gender or family structures.

We don't pretend to speak for all families. But it is our hope that anyone who has the privilege and responsibility of raising a child will benefit from our thinking, analysis, mistakes and triumphs. Read, ponder, take what works for you and your family, and discard what doesn't.

Introduction

Why we wrote this book

We are researchers, writers and parents. Since the birth of our first daughter, Violet, in 2009, we have been dedicated to finding out the best way to raise girls. In the beginning our investigation and analysis were for our own interest: we wanted to be the best parents we could possibly be. But as the years ticked by, people started asking us questions about our research and the way we apply it in our family. The parenting articles we have written for the media have garnered hundreds of thousands of comments and have been shared over ten million times. We have read countless parenting books and credible academic studies, attended parenting seminars and workshops, and interviewed experts the world over. Then one day at a kid's birthday party, we were discussing our research with other parents when a friend said, 'I don't have time to read all that. Can you just tell me what I need to do?'

That was the moment we realised we had to write this book, so that other parents who want to raise girls who like themselves can have easy access to all that we have learned from over a decade of study: as journalists we have the rare privilege of being able to call up the world's leading experts on parenting, psychology, education and development – something our friend at the party didn't have time for.

We have only included information and advice that we believe to be critical to raising girls who like themselves, and our emphasis is on steps that you can take immediately.

We are not going to make you feel bad. Honestly, there are not enough hours in the day to do everything you're expected to do to win the title of 'good parents'. Life is busy and complicated. Jobs need to be done and bills have to be paid. We both do paid work and we have no family support at all. All the strategies in this book have been successfully road-tested in our ordinary, imperfect family.

Not all of the advice contained in these pages is going to work for your family. Maybe it will inspire you to think of a different, and just as effective, approach that suits your unique situation. Or maybe not. Let's just agree from the outset that 'good-enough parents' is what we're aiming for. Although we offer you suggestions and strategies, this is a judgement-free zone.

Girls' report card

First, the good news. Our girls have more opportunities than their mothers and aunties. When it comes to education, they're smashing it in the classroom, outperforming boys at high school and university.

Young women are emboldened and capable of driving social change. The School Strike 4 Climate movement, which saw millions of kids all over the world go out in protest, was initiated by Swedish schoolgirl Greta Thunberg and organised primarily by young women.[1] Cairns schoolgirl Molly Steer is fighting to save the Great Barrier Reef and is successfully convincing local governments to ban single-use plastic straws.[2] Pakistani schoolgirl Malala Yousafzai was shot by the Taliban for fighting for the rights of girls to be educated, but now continues her work as a UN ambassador. Our girls have an abundance of great female role models – in industries such as music and sport and in activism – to inspire and empower them and to show them all the wonderful and varied ways to be a girl.

But – and it's an awfully big 'but' – far too many of our girls don't like themselves. Despite their numerous achievements and their competence, many struggle with confidence, resilience, emotional wellbeing and self-worth.[3] Below is a report card for the issues our daughters face.

Depression: F
Nearly 1 in 5 girls aged 16–17 meet the clinical criteria for depression.[4]

Anxiety: F
Seven per cent, or 1 in 14, of Australians aged 4–17 have experienced an anxiety disorder.[5] This figure only gets worse as our girls age, with 1 in 3 women in Australia experiencing anxiety.[6]

Self-harm: F
A quarter of girls aged 14–15 have had thoughts about self-harming in the previous 12 months[7] and one quarter of girls aged 16–17 told researchers that they had deliberately injured themselves at some point in their lives.[8]

Body image: F
The National Eating Disorders Collaboration found that more than 55 per cent of Australian girls aged 8–9 are dissatisfied with their body, and that by the ages of 10 and 11, 56 per cent of girls try to control their weight.[9]

Eating disorders: F
The Butterfly Foundation reports that eating disorders are the third most common chronic illness for young women. One in 10 people with anorexia nervosa do not live more than 10 years after the onset of the disorder.[10]

Body autonomy: F
Fifty-one per cent of girls say that they often feel pressured to take 'sexy' photos of themselves and share them. A survey conducted by Our Watch found that 62 per cent of girls and young women agreed that 'girls often feel pressured to take part in sexual activities with their boyfriend or husband'.[11]

This report card is enough to make any parent's blood run cold. It's a big part of why we are doing everything we can to build a solid foundation of self-worth while our daughters are young.

Why is this happening? Why are girls who appear to be swimming in a world of opportunity drowning in insecurity and self-loathing?

Because the world can be toxic for girls. We know that's a big claim, but the reality is that many girls are growing up in a society where they will be invisible if they don't act sexy, and be branded a slut if they do. The pressure to be thin and beautiful is so pervasive that we have heard stories of primary-school girls dreading going to school because they think that they look fat in their uniforms. And we're not talking upper primary school here. These girls are barely out of preschool.

Girls grow up being told that they can do anything they want in the world, but they often feel they must do it perfectly. There is no room for mistakes or flaws, no tolerance for imperfection. The fear of being embarrassed or judged can cripple girls' potential and steal their happiness.

Girls learn early that everything in life is a competition. They are told that their worth, beauty and achievements are only relative to those of the other girls around them, encouraging them to see their allies and friends as competitors and foes. Adults tell them they are powerful and then push them into a world that systematically disempowers them.

Whole industries are built on girls' fear of not living up to impossible expectations. Their self-worth is corroded bit by bit and then, when their insecurities are ratcheted all the way up, they are sold a supposed solution for a tidy sum.

With all of this going on, is it any wonder many girls blame themselves for not meeting people's expectations – and their own?

But it is we adults who are failing girls. And it is we parents who have the best chance of reversing this downward spiral.

A girl who likes herself

If the aim is to raise a girl who likes herself, what does success look like? There is no one way to be a girl, nor is there one way to like yourself. So how do we know specifically what we are trying to achieve and if we have reached our goal?

The following list of characteristics is a comprehensive picture of what a girl who likes herself must have. These are the foundational pillars your daughter needs to thrive in a world that is crushing so many of her peers. The following chapters will be devoted to each of these characteristics, exploring why they're important, what you can do to instil them within your daughter, and the obstacles that you may need to tackle.

1. A girl who likes herself has a power perspective.
2. A girl who likes herself has body confidence.
3. A girl who likes herself owns her body.
4. A girl who likes herself is calm.
5. A girl who likes herself is independent and masterful.
6. A girl who likes herself has strong relationships.
7. A girl who likes herself is herself.

You sound just like your mother!

Before we get to our girls, let's take a look in the mirror.

There is nothing like becoming a parent to open your eyes to how you were parented. You're barely home from hospital before words that you haven't heard since childhood start to tumble out of your mouth. Without warning, you hear yourself speaking like your own parents. Their baby talk, praise, criticism and songs fall effortlessly from your tongue. Values that you thought had died out with acid-wash jeans and prawn cocktails spring forth before your conscious thoughts have a chance to catch up. And that's when you have the realisation: 'I sound just like my mother/father!'

That may be a very good thing.

Maybe you had the best parents imaginable. Your parents may have been the kind that instilled in you a love of life, independence, and a large dose of empathy. If your kids turn out half as well as you then it will be high fives all round.

But for many of us, matters are a touch more complicated.

We're not about to suggest that your parents didn't do a good job, but the more conscious you are of the way you were parented, the more likely you are to make better decisions when it comes to raising your daughter. In some instances, you may be happy to parent in exactly the same way as your own parents did. In other cases you might want to make different choices. When you're aware of the baggage that you bring to parenting, you can make better choices about which parenting approaches you want to keep and which ones you'd like to ditch.

We have both tried to drop a lot of the baggage from our own childhoods. Some we have managed to ditch, much of it we haven't. But the good thing about being conscious of your baggage is that even though you may still carry it everywhere you go, you can choose not to unpack it in front of your kids.

Check your baggage

What is your baggage from childhood?

- Did you make your educational and career decisions based on following your own dreams and passion? Or did you do what you thought your parents wanted?

- Did you make your own relationship choices, or did you try to please your parents?
- Did your parents make you think you were already good enough, or did you have to be more or different to please them?
- Were mistakes allowed or encouraged in your family? Were your mistakes frowned upon and a source of tension between you and your parents? Did your parents ever acknowledge, apologise for or forgive their own mistakes?

What is your baggage as a parent?

- Are girls who are beautiful and thin better than those who are not?
- Should girls primarily be sweet and compliant?
- Do you secretly think men are smarter and more capable than women?
- Will you be disappointed if your daughter has different interests and values from your own?
- Do you sometimes make parenting decisions based on not wanting to feel embarrassed or judged by other parents, your partner, your own parents or in-laws, parenting 'experts' or even complete strangers?
- Do you think that gender stereotypes are 'natural' and therefore cannot be changed?
- Do you really 'just want your child to be happy'?
- Do you find yourself rewarding your daughter with more love and attention when she makes you proud?
- Is your daughter already good enough just the way she is?
- Do you secretly wish your daughter was a son?

A word to dads about dads

Many of you do not know how important you are.

People used to think that a father's job began and ended with being a good provider. Good provider = good father. They could not have been more wrong, and daughters have suffered because of this belief.

As an engaged and loving father, you can:

- boost your daughter's self-esteem and teach her to believe in herself
- hugely affect your daughter's choice of future partner
- be a positive influence on how your daughter views her body
- raise your daughter's academic performance
- teach your daughter critical thinking and self-reliance
- reduce the likelihood of your daughter developing an eating disorder, anxiety or depression.[12]

The research is in and there is no doubt about it: good dads make great daughters. But having never been a girl, and perhaps never even playing with them as kids, some dads can be unsure where to start. We have written this book for dads just as much as we have for mums. But we've noticed that, for a variety of reasons, the dads we know are less likely to read parenting books than mothers. If this is not true for you, please read on. If this does apply to you, you can flick to the end of each chapter, where we have listed actions for dads to take that will have an enormous influence on raising your girl to like herself. We know you're busy, but go back a couple of pages to the Girls' Report Card and think about what is at stake. Spending a couple of minutes at the end of each chapter reading the 'Action For Dads' section could give you some tips and strategies to make a vital difference to your daughter's life.

1

A girl who likes herself has a power perspective

The power of the flyscreen door

Did you ever play the flyscreen game as a child? No?

For those whose childhoods were a little more exciting than ours, the rules – if you can call them that – are pretty simple. To play the game, focus on the screen door and notice the grime and occasional dead insect. Focus hard enough and that's all you see. Then soften your gaze and shift perspective to look past the screen to the outside. If you do this for long enough, the world outside eventually comes into focus and you won't see the flyscreen anymore: the barrier, the constraint, the dirt and the dead bugs disappear as the world beyond comes into view with crystal clarity.

The flyscreen door game is a practical lesson in the power of perception. It teaches that you see what you focus on. And what you focus on, you see. You can choose to see the screen that limits you. Or you can choose to look at the world of possibilities beyond it.

The screen door game is all very Zen (with a suburban twist). But what does it have to do with raising girls?

Quite a lot, as it happens.

What you focus on frames how you see – and respond to – the world. Two people can be faced with exactly the same situation and yet have totally opposite responses to it depending on their perspective.

Take the following example. Two girls go off to school camp for the first time. Both are equally capable. They are going to exactly the same place with exactly the same people. They'll do the same activities, eat the same food, sleep in the same tents, stay up to past their bedtime eating too many lollies, and annoy their teachers to about the same degree.

But their attitudes are anything but similar. One child bounds onto the bus, so full of beans she almost forgets to give her parents a kiss goodbye. The second child, meanwhile, is fearful and anxious. She's crying, hyperventilating, clinging, and needs to be dragged from her mother's leg to get on the bus.

All else being equal, a key reason for the difference in these girls' behaviour comes down to perspective. The first girl has what we call a power perspective. She's not afraid of the unknown because she believes that she has the inner strength and capabilities to deal with whatever happens on camp. The second girl, despite having the same capabilities, feels powerless, is terrified by the unknown and is worried she won't be able to cope.

A big part of raising girls who like themselves is helping them to develop a power perspective. It's the difference between feeling crushed by 'the biggest mistake of your life' versus seeing mistakes as inevitable, another opportunity to learn and do better next time. It's standing at the foot of the mountain, thinking it's insurmountable so there is no point trying, versus thinking that you'd better get started because it might take a while. Someone with a power perspective, or what psychologists call an internal locus of control, believes that they are largely responsible for how they respond to the world.[1] They believe that the setbacks in their life are temporary and manageable. They bounce back quickly from these setbacks because they are certain that they can solve – or at least confront – their problems.[2] Rather than being dragged down by their current situation or circumstances, they seek to change them.

People who have a power perspective approach life confident that they can give anything a try. Note that word 'try'. They're not assured of success. Life won't necessarily go to plan. In fact, life may very well go pear-shaped. And the pear in question may be shaped like the one that's forgotten at the bottom of your daughter's schoolbag, rotting. But even when things go wrong in their lives, as they inevitably will, people with a power perspective still believe that they will be okay. People who have a power perspective back themselves. They trust their own judgement, rather than deferring to peers and powerful others or believing that life is determined by luck/bad luck and chance.

People with a power perspective worry a whole lot less because they believe that, even when things don't turn out the way they want, they can influence the outcomes in their lives. On those occasions when they can't control the outcomes (such as the death of a loved one, illness, injustice) they believe that they have the internal strength and capabilities to deal with whatever comes their way.

There are many reasons why a power perspective is important and beneficial to girls, which we'll get to later in this chapter. But perhaps the most significant one is that a power perspective is just that: a perspective. It's not reality. It's the stories we tell ourselves about reality. It's how we describe the world to ourselves. It's what we think is important. It's whose opinions we think count. It's seeing the glass half full versus half empty. Same glass, same contents. But it's a completely different way of looking at it. Everything we experience is filtered through our own interpretations and descriptions of the world.

If our girls don't view the world from a power perspective, then in some ways it doesn't matter what reality throws at them.

3

Whether it's good or bad, they will interpret it from a perspective of powerlessness. If everyday setbacks crush them or if they see their future through a haze of negativity, then they will approach the future with fear and trepidation. Similarly, if they achieve amazing successes, but they believe their achievements are nothing more than dumb luck or that they fall short of their perfectionist standards, then they may well also believe they are failures.

This is why perspective is so foundational to raising a girl who likes herself. In this chapter we are going to show you how to foster a power perspective in your daughter, so she grows up optimistic, brave and self-reliant.

The power of the power perspective

As we have already said, a power perspective is about perception. It's not about reality itself. But this perspective – the way our girls approach the world – has very real consequences for their health and wellbeing. Children who have a power perspective – or an internal locus of control – are likely to not only have a happier childhood, but also exhibit higher self-esteem as adults.[3] Unsurprisingly, people who have a power perspective are more resilient and tend to be more successful than people who feel powerless in their lives. They work harder because they believe their hard work will pay off and that they will eventually achieve their goals, even though they will deal with setbacks along the way.

And the benefits of a power perspective go beyond the psychological. Adopting a power perspective can also improve people's physical wellbeing. For example, optimistic and empowered adults are less likely to have heart attacks[4] and have lower rates of mortality from all causes.[5] They develop fewer colds and flus[6] and have less inflammation.[7]

The opposite of an internal locus of control is (you guessed it) an external locus of control. People with an external locus of control believe that their lives are largely determined by chance events, faith, luck or other people who are more powerful than them. These other powerful people could be teachers or parents, but they can also be influential peers, celebrities and social media influencers or advertisers.

People who view the world from a perspective of powerlessness tend to be pessimistic and prone to feelings of helplessness. They also tend to suffer from depression more readily than people with a power perspective. They are more likely to underachieve at school and don't do so well in the workplace. Their relationships are often less stable.[8] If our girls have an external locus of control they will be more likely to experience panic disorders,[9] anxiety and depression, since they do not believe that they are in control of their lives.[10] If you don't have faith that you can cope with life's twists and turns then the world will be very scary indeed. The tragedy of a helpless perspective is that it prevents people from taking steps to make their situation better. What's the point of trying if you believe you're going to fail and that everything is going to turn to shit anyway?

A power perspective isn't New Age crap

To be blunt, the idea of a power perspective isn't just a rehash of the usual self-help nonsense that says that you, and you alone, control your life. A power perspective is not about simply putting positive thoughts out into the universe and then sitting back, doing nothing and waiting for the universe to give you 'abundance', as some self-help gurus like to pretend. In fact, when you think about it, the idea that the universe is going to magically give you what you want is precisely the opposite of having a power perspective because it still assumes that an external force controls your life. Of course, adopting a power perspective doesn't guarantee success. But it does tip the odds in favour of success, for the simple reason that people who think they have a chance of getting what they want are more likely to act in ways that may lead to success.

What's your perspective?

Quiz time! One of the first steps to raising a girl with a power perspective is to discover how you see the world. Respond to the following statements as honestly as you can. If your daughter is old enough, you can ask her to do the same to find out how she views the world.

When you do well on a test you:

A. Attribute your success to your own abilities and hard work.
B. Put it down to luck, an easy test or that the teacher liked you.

If someone criticises your work you:

A. Decide for yourself the quality of your work.
B. Figure that they must know more than you and think about how to change your work.

In a new and unknown situation you:

A. Feel excited stepping into the unknown, confident that what-ever happens you'll be okay.
B. Worry about everything that could go wrong and stress about how you are going to cope.

When you make a mistake you:

A. Learn from it so you can do better next time, and then move on.
B. Take it as proof that you're a bit hopeless and feel bad about yourself.

If you answered A to all of the above, you have a power perspec-tive. You believe you have the power to influence what happens in your life. Answering B to some of the questions indicates that you feel helpless and powerless in some aspects of your life. It doesn't mean that you are less capable or skilled than the people who answered A – you just *think* you are.

Born this way?

All of these benefits of having a power perspective are great if you and your daughter already have an internal locus of control and an optimistic outlook. But what if that's not the case? What if, on the contrary, your daughter is prone to seeing the world as a scary place? Was she just born this way and will she feel powerless forever?

The good news is that our perspective is not fixed. A growing body of evidence shows that it is possible to modify our perspective. This applies to both children and adults.[11] Children are even better than adults at learning how to reverse their unhelpful thinking and cultivating a power perspective. Remember, a power perspective is just that: a *perspective*. It's not reality. Just as you can change your view of something by shifting your focus, you can change how you see the world by deciding to look at life differently. You can train yourself – and your daughter – to approach life with a power perspective. The kinds of attitudes and predispositions that create a power perspective can be learned; they can be nurtured.

Admittedly, that's more easily said than done. We certainly don't want to suggest that those who don't have a power perspective are simply choosing to look at the world in a way that disempowers them. There may be very good reasons that your daughter, or you, views the world this way. You may have experienced terrible pain and loss. Getting over that isn't a walk in the park. And most likely, no one has ever taught you how to develop a power perspective. A power perspective is a skill, just like any other, but, unlike learning to read, it is rarely a focus in children's education.

To be absolutely clear, people with a power perspective didn't win the genetic lottery. They weren't born more intelligent, skilful or capable than people with an external locus of control. Nor are their lives trouble- or problem-free. They experience pain, frustration, failure and hardship as much as everyone else. It's just that they have found a more helpful perspective on their reality. They think in a way that works in their favour, rather than against them.

Developing a power perspective

Like most things in life, a power perspective doesn't happen in one big life-defining moment. It's the little, unremarkable daily events that have the most impact. We keep an eye out for everyday opportunities for our girls to develop and practise their power perspective.

Choosing a focus

We teach our girls that they have the power to choose their experience based on what they focus on. They can focus on all that's positive in their life and feel good, or they can focus on the negatives and feel bad. There are some things in life that really are awful and will make anyone miserable, but a lot of the time it is a choice. We tell them that they have the power to change their thoughts, change their perspective and choose to feel good about themselves and their life.

For example, one year Ivy accidentally broke one of Violet's birthday presents. To make matters worse, it was just minutes after she'd unwrapped it. As you can imagine, there were lots of tears. Our first instinct was to tell Violet that we'd buy her another toy, but while this would have minimised her distress in the short-term, rushing in to rescue her would have diminished her power perspective.

Instead, we gave Violet the opportunity to express her feelings of anger and sadness. We told her that, yes, it was disappointing that her toy was broken, but it was something that couldn't be changed. But what she did have the power to change was her perspective. She could choose to focus on the broken present and feel sad for the rest of the day, or she could choose to think about all the good that had happened – her party, her other presents, all the people who love her and wanted to celebrate her birthday with her. She had the power to decide if she wanted to spend the rest of her birthday feeling happy and grateful or sad.

'Focus on what you have, rather than on what you don't have' is a key message for our girls. It becomes especially handy when they come home wanting to collect the latest little plastic junk that is just a child's attention span away from ending up as landfill. On these occasions we tell our girls that they can focus on the toys they don't have – and that we're not going to buy – and feel miserable, or they can think about all the lovely toys they do have and feel grateful and content.

The larger lesson is that emotions don't just happen. It might seem like you suddenly feel bad for no reason, or an external event makes you feel awful. This could be a comment or look from another person, or a disappointing mark on a test. But there is a step in between the triggering event and the feeling, and that is the thought you have about the event. It is how you *perceive* the event that determines how you feel about it.[12] For example, think back to the girls going on school camp. Imagine they arrive at the camp site only to discover that they can't sleep in the same cabin as their best friend. The girl with the power perspective might feel temporarily disappointed, but then decide this is an opportunity to make new friends. Even if she doesn't, she'll still get to see her bestie during the day. The girl without the power perspective may be distressed by the change in sleeping arrangements, and take it as proof that camp really is awful and that she is definitely going to have a terrible time and hate every minute of it. The same situation can buoy one girl and crush another, and the difference is how they thought about it.

The key to cultivating a power perspective is understanding the relationship between thoughts and emotions. Our feelings follow our thoughts. When confronted with the change of cabin on camp, the girl with the power perspective *thought* that this could be an opportunity to make friends. Even if it wasn't, she *thought* she would still have fun during the day. As a result, she *felt* happy, content and excited. By contrast, the girl without the power perspective *thought* that the change in sleeping arrangements was evidence that camp was going from bad to worse. These thoughts most likely triggered *feelings* of unhappiness and anxiety.

If we can train our girls to have more positive and empowered thoughts, they will have more positive and empowering emotions.

Prioritising positive thoughts

One proven way to start developing a girl's power perspective is the 'What Went Well' exercise.[13] For this exercise, all you need to do is set aside ten minutes before you go to sleep to write down three things that went well in the day. Then add in why they went well. Your list needn't be filled with earth-shattering achievements. You don't have to have discovered a cure for cancer, won an Academy Award, or solved the climate crisis. Something as simple as 'We had a lovely family dinner tonight because I made it a priority' is great. From your child's point of view, it could be 'I helped Mum cook dinner and it was yum.' You don't need to ask your girls each night to make a list of what went well. Instead, prompt them often to think in terms of what went well. After school pick-up, for example, ask, 'What was the best thing that happened today?' Follow up by asking them why it was good and what role they played in making it good. At the end of each school term, school year, weekend or holiday, we ask these same questions.

Acknowledging even seemingly small, everyday achievements is a way of training your daughter to think more optimistically by focusing on positive events, rather than constantly defaulting to the negative. Psychologist Martin Seligman, who came up with the 'What Went Well' exercise and has forty-five years of research and clinical studies under his belt, says that if you do this exercise for a week, 'the odds are you will be less depressed, happier and addicted to this exercise six months from now'.

Kasey's story

I have my own version of the 'What Went Well' exercise that I have been using successfully for years to develop and maintain my power perspective. I jokingly call it my FIGJAM list (as in, Fuck I'm Good; Just Ask Me), which I learned from a book called *Thrive* by Rob Kelly.[14]

It works like this: I keep a list on my phone of the good things that happen in my life and what this says about me. I also imagine what my best friend would say if I told her about them. For example, I might write, 'I had a really productive writing day. I wrote 1000 words.' And then I'd imagine my friend's response and write it down, such as, 'Well done. You're a really hard worker and your book will be finished in no time.' Another example might be, 'I went to the gym today even though I didn't want to. Well done, I'm taking care of myself.'

I add to this list and read it most days. When I am feeling low or if I feel myself regressing back into my old unhelpful and disempowered thinking pattern, I read the list. I'll read it on the tram, when I'm waiting to pick up my girls and when I take breaks at my desk.

I started using this exercise several years ago when I made a conscious choice to change my external locus of control into a power perspective. I had grown up defaulting to the opinions of my parents, peers and then bosses, and even random strangers, to determine if I was worthy and if my work was good enough. I was a little girl in a grown woman's body, still waiting for the elephant stamp to confirm that I was a Good Girl (more on this on page 184). I can say, without hesitation, that my FIGJAM list helps me control my thoughts so I can live a life that is more empowered.

It seems too simple to work, childish even. But the benefits for my thinking and my wellbeing have been profound and enduring. I see that passing on this skill to my girls is a gift that they can unwrap every day of their lives.

Powerful praise

A crucial factor in the success of the What Went Well exercise is agency. Talking about nice deeds that other people do or chance events is lovely but it won't build a power perspective. A power perspective comes from within – it's what your daughter did for herself that matters. This same focus on agency is critical when it comes to the way we praise our girls. If we do it well, we can strengthen their power perspective and help prevent them from becoming praise junkies.

It's normal for girls to seek out praise from their parents and other adults. They'll show us their paintings, their Lego creations, their school assignments and ask, 'Do you like it?' The answer (if we're being honest) usually goes something like, 'That's lovely, sweetie,' while what's going through our mind is, 'Ummm, what is it?' Our inclination as parents is to tell our children that they, and everything they produce, is wonderful.

But enthusiastically approving of your child's every achievement isn't necessarily doing them any favours when it comes to building a power perspective. The reason is that it validates their seeking of approval from someone else. In doing so, it reinforces the notion that other people's opinions are more important than their own. In the process, it can be detrimental to your daughter developing a power perspective.

But there is a way to give praise, while also encouraging her power perspective. Here's how: rather than simply praising her work, take the opportunity to turn her question around and direct it back at her. When she asks you, 'Do you like my dress/dance/somersault/artwork?', flip the question around and ask her, 'Do *you* like your dress/dance/somersault/artwork?'

If our daughter says 'yes' then we tell her that it's her work, so her opinion matters most and she should be proud of herself. If she says 'no', we then talk about what she'd like to do differently next time and the importance of practising.

In the larger scheme of things, it might not sound that significant. But think of how many times each week your child comes to you seeking praise. This quickly adds up to thousands of opportunities to teach a power perspective and subtly tell your daughter that her opinions about her achievements, behaviour and appearance matter more than anybody else's – even yours.

De-escalate the catastrophe

Along with praise-seeking, another everyday occurrence that can either build or corrode a girl's power perspective is how we deal with catastrophising.

Catastrophising is making small stuff (and sometimes even big stuff) seem far worse than it is in reality. Girls, especially, are often rewarded for catastrophising. They can get a lot of attention for acting weak and fragile. Look around a playground and you will see girls cry when they are not particularly hurt because they get special attention. They'll fake their fear because they get even more attention when they are rescued. These behaviours are often played out in TV shows and movies where female characters are often squealy and passive. When our girls spend time watching other girls catastrophise, whether on TV or in the playground, they are also more likely to act more fragile and powerless than they normally do.

You can easily tell when someone's catastrophising by the words they use. Listen out for words like 'can't', 'worst', 'never', 'always', 'devastated' and 'everyone'. They'll say, 'I'm the worst at drawing unicorns,' 'I'll never be able to win this game,' or 'Everyone can skip/throw/run better than me.' These are 'absolute' words, in the sense that they *absolutely* block out other ways of seeing or interpreting events. 'Always' means there are no exceptions – not a single one. 'Never' is never again. 'Everyone' includes, well, everyone on the planet. 'Worst' means that there has never been anyone or anything as bad.

When girls use these words, they remove the possibility of seeing things differently or seeing how they could be different in the future. And because absolute words rule out other possibilities, they have the effect of magnifying problems and making our girls feel alone and powerless to change the situation that they find themselves in. They become hapless victims of external events beyond their control.

Averting catastrophic thinking

A great way to challenge catastrophic thinking is to question the absolute words our girls use – and begin to unpick them. One way to do this is to remind your daughter that whatever catastrophe she's experiencing is temporary. If our girls say they had the 'worst' day 'ever', we pull them up on it. Was their day really the *worst* day *ever*? Or was it just a pretty ordinary day, but there's always tomorrow? Similarly, rather than letting our daughter get caught up in the idea that she's 'the worst' at drawing (or whatever), we help her to reframe it so that she locates her experience in time. For example, 'I'm terrible at maths' can be reframed to 'I struggle with maths at the moment, but I'm practising'. This is actually a more accurate statement about her abilities than the absolute words she has used. It also lowers the pitch of catastrophic thinking, making it clear that whatever her current challenge, it is temporary and, crucially, it can be changed if she chooses to work at it. Point out that there have been lots of things in her life that she found really hard to start with but, by practising, she can now do with ease. That might apply to writing her name, reading, riding a bike or scooter, or playing Minecraft.

Absolute words also tend to be global in their scope: they apply to everyone and everything. And because they apply universally, they have the capacity to infect every sphere of life, colouring how girls view themselves and their abilities. A girl can believe that one setback in one specific area of her life is positive proof that she is doomed to fail in other areas of her life as well. For example, 'I can't read as well as my friend, I'm dumb.' You can help your daughter to reframe the catastrophe by focusing on the specific, rather than the global. Perhaps your daughter can't read as well as her friend, *yet*. But with time and practice she will probably catch up. And even if she doesn't, does that make her dumb at everything else?

If she complains that 'everyone is better than me at sport', ask whether everyone includes everyone in the whole world. Ask her if that applies to all sports. Surely there is some sport, or some aspect of the sport in question, that she's good at or has the capacity to get better at with time and practice.

Give more attention to getting up than falling down

Of course, there will be times when girls need our support and care for their legitimate fears and injuries. The trick is to distinguish the real concerns from the performances of weakness to get special treatment or because of a mistaken belief that this behaviour is expected of girls. As a general rule, we give our girls more attention as a reward for their strengths and courage, rather than their weaknesses. We validate them when they try, and when they show persistence and courage. When they stumble we don't say, 'You fell over, oh dear,' we say, 'You got back up, well done.'

Just as we teach our kids to tie their shoelaces and to say please and thank you, we can also teach them how to think. If our girls are going to develop a power perspective, then we need to take conscious steps to reject the damsel in distress stereotype that is so often presented to them. We have to spend time explaining to our girls that if they *act* as if they are powerless and incapable, their brain will start to believe they actually *are* powerless and incapable. You can have an enormous influence on your daughter's perspective.

When you wish upon a star . . . nothing happens

At the opposite end of the spectrum from catastrophising is making wishes. Girls, from a young age, are encouraged to make wishes. Countless toys, books and TV shows aimed at girls centre around the idea that making wishes is the key to success and happiness. My Little Pony has a book titled *Wishes Do Come True*, Barbie has a book called *Ballet Wishes* and a Birthday Wishes doll, and there are endless varieties of fairy 'wish kits'.

On the surface, making wishes might seem to indicate the ultimate in optimism. But in terms of developing a power perspective, wishing is just as damaging as catastrophising. Both position girls as being at the mercy of external forces that they cannot control. The only difference is that with wishes, those external forces – imagined or real – view your daughter in a kindly way, whereas in catastrophic thinking the external forces are malevolent. Wishing encourages girls to sit quietly and hope that someone else will meet their needs, rather than taking on that initiative, control and responsibility themselves.

Contrast the focus on wishes for girls with the way we treat boys. Toys that are pushed at boys, for example, are mostly about action and adventure. Boys' playtime is packed chock-full of opportunities to act out being agents in their lives, rather than waiting passively for someone else to intervene and grant their desires.

Not convinced that wishes are disempowering? Then consider the grown-up version of wishing. Think about the woman who hopes that her boss will recognise her contribution and talent and give her a pay rise, rather than building a compelling case for the raise and then going in and asking for it. Another version of grown-up wishing is sticking a picture of a dream house on a vision board and thinking that's all that is required to magically manifest it, instead of also putting in the time and effort to develop and commit to a savings and investment plan. It's 'putting it out there into the universe' versus backing yourself and working for it.

Of course, there is nothing inherently wrong with playing games about wishing and magic. We encourage our girls to make wishes when they cut their birthday cakes, the same as any other parents. But wishing is a problem when it becomes a girl's default way of thinking about the world. When our girls make wishes we tell them that wishes *do* come true – if you work for them. We prompt them to think about what they are going to do to make their wish come true, rather than allowing them to sit back and expect it to just happen while doing nothing.

Hinting versus asking

Another more subtle way girls are encouraged to be powerless, which they are sometimes rewarded for, is to hint rather than ask. They'll say, 'I'm hungry,' 'I'm thirsty,' 'It's broken,' or 'It's lost,' rather than coming out and asking for what they want. These are passive ways of engaging with the world. They're not even requests for someone else to fix the problem. In these cases, girls simply put a fact out there and hope – or expect – that someone else will a) come up with a solution, and b) deliver that solution. Here, an external force is required to solve their problems. This is a passive mindset, far away from the power perspective we're seeking to instil in girls.

If your girl does tend to hint rather than ask, encourage her to reframe her thinking about problems into solutions. For example, when our girls say, 'I'm hungry,' we answer with the dad joke, 'Hi, Hungry! Nice to see you.' When they follow up with an exasperated, 'No! I'm HUNGRY!' we tell them, 'That's the problem, so what's the solution?' Soon enough they will get the point and reply, 'Can I have something to eat, please?'

Girls with a power perspective can be just as hopeful and optimistic as other girls, but their hope is built on their sense of their own agency rather than a passive acceptance of what is, or an inability to assert what they actually want. Instead of sprinkling fairy dust and making a wish, or talking around what they want, the hope and optimism of girls with a power perspective stems from their confidence: confidence in their own abilities; confidence to articulate their wants and needs; confidence that their determination and hard work are most likely to get them what they want.

Avoid judgement

They say there are two certainties in life: death and taxes. But there is one other certainty: judgement. No matter what you do, how hard you try, or how good you are, some form of judgement is inevitable. When it comes to judgement, developing your daughter's fledgling power perspective may require a rethink of your own parenting. How many times when you were growing up did you hear phrases such as 'You're embarrassing yourself', 'You'll look silly', 'Stop showing off'? And how many times have you found yourself repeating these words as a parent?

For example, we once saw a grandmother at the park with her granddaughter, who was around two years old. The little girl had eaten a tub of yoghurt and, unsurprisingly, had smeared it all over her face. She was eager to resume playing in the sandpit, but her grandmother insisted on cleaning her up first.

'We have to clean your face,' Grandma said. 'What will people think if they see you with a messy face?'

We believe that most parenting comes from love and the best intentions. Managing a child's behaviour by making them self-conscious is no exception. But those words 'What will people think?' can rob girls of the opportunity to develop a power perspective. These kinds of statements train girls to be acutely and constantly aware of other people's judgements of them.

Another example of a common parenting line that teaches self-consciousness is, 'Stop the tantrum because people are looking at you.'

Parents usually make comments like this because they are trying to be considerate of the people around them, and they want their child to learn to do the same. But children absorb not just the content of our criticism (you shouldn't have a dirty face) but also the substance of it (because people will judge you and that matters).[15] Repeated over time, children start to assume that people are always looking at them and judging them – even when they're not. (Most often, people are far more interested in their own lives than they are in anyone else's.) This constant focus on what other people think swells to a wave with a pull so strong it can drag in every interaction a girl will have with the world.

It's hard to imagine how a girl can ever feel truly content and secure if she has been trained to believe that other people's opinions about her matter more than her own. Other people can be insensitive or outright cruel, they might have their own agendas, but more than anything they are inconsistent. You never really know what response you're going to get from people, so if a girl grows up believing that other people's responses define her worth, then she will end up living in a state of constant insecurity. Her life may always feel out of control because she has been taught that her fate is in the hands of other people.

Building a power perspective in girls begins with instilling in them a robust sense of themselves. That may mean unlearning some of the ways that we ourselves were parented. How can a child develop a robust sense of self and confidence if we make them hyper aware and fearful of other people's judgement? How can they ever feel secure if we teach them that complete strangers have the power to decide if they are good or bad? One of the most empowering gifts we can give to our girls – far more important and enduring than a clean face at the park – is teaching them to trust their own judgement, rather than giving that power to others.

Just to be clear, we're not suggesting that we should raise our girls to be rude and inconsiderate. Nor are we suggesting that girls should be raised contrary to everyday social norms just for the sake of it. We are not saying that we should let our kids scream in cafes (although as every parent knows, despite our very best efforts this is sometimes unavoidable). We put a lot of effort into raising children who are considerate of other people, but there is a difference between being considerate of other people and deferring to other people's opinions to dictate your behaviour or your worth. Girls who like themselves learn to be kind and considerate because it is in line with their own values, not because they fear being judged by others.

Chris's story

When Violet was a preschooler she went through her Elsa stage. She would walk down the street screeching 'Let it go' at the top of her voice. When she attempted her Elsa rendition in a cafe or a crowded place, I would tell her to be quiet by explaining that other people were busy with their own conversations or having silent alone time and didn't want to listen to her. I reinforced her power perspective by focusing on her ability to choose to be a kind and considerate person, rather than disempowering her by teaching her that she needed to change her behaviour because other people would judge her.

When Violet and I would go for walks around our neighbourhood, she would also sing her Elsa songs. Given the volume, or perhaps Violet's sheer joy and exuberance, people did indeed look at her. She was oblivious to this and I was sure not to mention it. Violet was not hurting or inconveniencing anyone with her singing. So I encouraged her happiness, self-expression and confidence. 'Sing louder,' I'd say. Had I told her that other people were looking at her and that she should stop singing, I would have laid a brick of self-consciousness and social anxiety into the foundation of her growing identity.

Dealing with criticism

One of the keys to developing your daughter's power perspective is teaching her how to deal with the judgement of others, particularly criticism. Some kids appear to be naturally thicker-skinned and more robust than others; criticism seems to bounce off them. But if girls become fearful of criticism, they end up living half-lives, avoiding situations where they might be criticised, or being inauthentic because they fear that showing their true self will invite criticism.

Regardless of your daughter's current disposition, all kids can develop skills to deal with criticism. Just like any skill, our girls will get better at dealing with criticism with practice. One approach we've adopted is based on the work of Brené Brown, a US social scientist and author who studies shame and vulnerability.

One of Brown's most important insights is that criticism is inevitable. That might seem obvious, but it's often overlooked. It doesn't matter how good you are or how hard you try, criticism is a fact of life.

Think about who cops criticism in life. High on the list are athletes, politicians, artists, princesses. But you don't have to be in the public eye to be criticised. Show us the person who organised your school raffle and we bet that someone said they could have done better. The captain of your daughter's netball team, the lead in her school play, and the kid who spoke at assembly all copped flak from someone. In fact, anyone who does anything out of the ordinary or who puts themselves out there gets criticised by someone.

Put like that, it sounds really bleak and depressing. It might make you want to wrap your daughter up and hide her from all the pain in the world. But teaching your daughter that criticism is an unavoidable part of life is a gift, because in time she will come to realise that criticism is not personal. It's not about her, or her work. Anyone who chooses to live a life that is big and bold, or who does anything creative, or who swims outside the flags of life is going to be criticised. We need to teach our girls that criticism is the entry price to living the life they want.

We are not saying we shouldn't care at all about what other people think. We're not talking about constructive criticism, the kind of feedback that makes us better. But there is nothing to be gained from listening to people who just want to kick you in the guts. It's easy to sit on the sidelines of life and sling mud. With social media, our girls are growing up in a world where they could potentially be exposed to haters 24/7. Our job is to teach them to know the difference between people they should listen to and those they can safely ignore.

We have two simple techniques to help with this, one for younger girls and one for older girls.

For younger girls: the giraffe

When our girls come to us to report that someone has said something mean about them, such as 'Joe said I was stupid' or 'Katie said I'm a big baby', we reply, 'If Joe/Katie said you were a giraffe, would that make you a giraffe?'

This question provokes a laugh, or at the very least a smile, so it's great for defusing the emotion. But it's also something that even young children can understand. They are not a giraffe no matter who says they are.

When our girls have composed themselves after our hilarious giraffe gag, we explain that it doesn't matter what Joe or Katie says, it doesn't make it true. We then reiterate our power perspective lesson, that they get to decide who they are and what they are like. Their opinion of themselves is what matters most.

For older girls: a card trick

We learned this card trick from Brené Brown, who carries a similar card in her wallet to keep criticism in perspective. Get a piece of card, small enough to fit in your pocket – a piece of cardboard the size of a business card is ideal. On the card, write the names of six people whose opinions matter to you and whose criticism you will choose to listen to.

In deciding whose names are written on our cards, Brown suggests applying the following criteria:

1. Do they show up? Unless this person is also putting themselves out there, being brave, we shouldn't listen to them.
2. Do they have your best interests at heart? Are they being critical because they genuinely want to help you be better, or do they want to hurt you, mock you, or silence you?
3. Do you respect them? Do they know what they are talking about?

The best thing about the card trick is that your daughter has to think about who in her life has earned the right to be listened to. Yes, these are external people. But she knows why she is listening to these people, and not the many other voices around her.

If you receive criticism from someone who is not on your card, and they don't deserve to be added to your card, you disregard their feedback. Of course, no one is made of Teflon. There are times when a person's criticism can break through our defences. On these occasions, tell your daughter to speak to someone who is on her card to get their perspective.

Action for dads

Your daughter cares a lot about what you think. Use that influence to help her develop a power perspective by teaching her that she should care about what *she* thinks. When she comes to you asking for your opinion about her artwork/dance/dress, flip the question and instead ask her what she thinks. When she asks for your advice or assistance, pause for a moment before helping her and encourage her to first try to work it out herself.

Recap

- A power perspective is just that: a perspective. It's the way your daughter looks at the world and her relationship with it. Does she see problems or opportunities? Is she crushed by a mistake or does she bounce back, stronger and more determined? Does she think that she can influence what happens in her life or is everything decided by fate, chance, luck or powerful people such as parents, teachers or peers?
- People with a power perspective tend to be bolder and less fearful because they believe they have the inner strength and capabilities to deal with life. They also work harder because they believe that they can achieve what they want through

their efforts. They also tend to be physically and emotionally healthier.

- A power perspective can be learned with practice. If your daughter does not currently have a power perspective, you can help her develop one through everyday opportunities such as reminding her that her opinion about herself matters more than anyone else's (even yours), focusing on the 'getting up' rather than the 'falling down', breaking down and challenging catastrophic language and wishful thinking, and incorporating the 'What Went Well' exercise into your daily conversations.

2

A girl who likes herself has body confidence

The scene is a mothers' group meeting. An eighteen-month-old girl crawls on a floor strewn with toys and other toddlers. A worn plastic plate of cupcakes is being passed around by the natural organiser of the group – the mother who remembers everyone's birthdays, arranges the meetings and brings the food.

One mother refuses the plate. 'I can't have any,' she says. 'They're two points each and I've already had too many points today.' She's doing Weight Watchers in an attempt to lose her baby weight.

Another mum pipes up. 'I can't have any either. I've been such a pig today.'

And faster than you can say 'body shame', the weight comments go viral around the room. Almost all of the women find a reason not to take a cupcake. The few who do add the obligatory self-incriminating comments about their lack of self-control or the standard 'diet starts tomorrow' quip. The plate returns to a table as the conversation turns to weight gain and weight loss.

There's a name for these conversations: it's called 'fat chat'. Chatting about weight – whether congratulating other women for losing weight or commiserating with them for gaining pounds (or staying the same) – is a way that women have been taught to bond. Women use weight to start conversations and strengthen their relationships, and the script is almost always the same. Women tell other women that they have nothing to worry about. That they, in fact, are the ones who need to lose a few kilos. They think they are building each other up, but research shows that they are actually making everyone involved feel worse. Women who engage in fat chat come away from these kinds of exchanges with lower body satisfaction.[1]

But the women participating in the fat chat in the mothers' group meeting aren't the only ones being hurt by it. Their children are too. Girls, in particular, are watching and learning from their mothers.

Before these toddlers are old enough to walk away, before they are able to question the insanity of it all, these little girls are listening to women congratulating themselves for losing weight or criticising themselves because they haven't. These girls are learning, quite literally at their mother's knees, that mummy should deprive herself, that she is too fat – and that it matters.

And unless something changes, these girls will most likely grow up hating their own bodies as much as their mothers have learned to hate theirs. As these girls become women, they will believe that their bodies, and other people's assessments of their beauty, will define their worth in the world. They will let a number on the scales dictate what sort of day they'll have, and their main use of maths could quite possibly become counting Weight Watchers points.

Body insecurity is not natural

Countless studies show that the vast majority of women are dissatisfied with their bodies, but they didn't start out feeling this way. Girls are not born hating their bodies. Watch young children play or look at themselves in the mirror and you will see them marvel at all their body can do. Body hatred is not innate; it is taught to girls in their homes, in their schools and peer groups, every time they switch on the TV, or get onto social media, or leave the house. From the time they open their eyes in the morning to the time they go to sleep at night, girls will learn that their body is flawed.

Unless we intervene.

Imagine for a moment how much better life would be for the women you know, and perhaps yourself, if they could sail through their day without constant body hatred clogging their thoughts and dragging them down. Now imagine if you could give that freedom to your daughter. In many cases, it would be life-changing.

We need to make a conscious decision to do everything we can to stop our girls learning to hate and mistrust their bodies. We need to help them develop the foundation and skills to reject the constant messages of body hatred when we are not around to protect them.

This chapter details strategies to inoculate our girls against learning to hate their bodies.

Why body confidence is important

It's tempting to write off body issues as little more than yet another obsession of the Instagram generation. It's just vanity. Or it's shallowness. The seemingly timeless focus on body and weight can be rationalised as just 'girls' stuff'. It's 'girls being girls', something that girls do, and we can't do anything about it.

But body hatred is not trivial. More than 55 per cent of Australian girls between the ages of 8 and 9 are dissatisfied with their body. By the ages of 10 and 11, 56 per cent of girls are trying to control their weight.[2] The National Eating Disorders Collaboration advises that '[t]he act of starting *any* diet increases the risk of eating disorders' (our emphasis).[3]

Sadly, eating disorders are not well understood. The seriousness of diseases such as anorexia are downplayed as nothing more than extreme dieting or taking dieting too far. In some cases, people even express envy about anorexia, joking that they wish they had an eating disorder so they could lose a few kilos. They're kidding, of course, but imagine saying that you wanted another serious mental illness, such as depression.

The bottom line is that eating disorders are life-threatening illnesses. Eating disorders kill people. In fact, your daughter has a greater chance of dying from an eating disorder than of being abducted by a stranger on the street. Despite this, we spend way more time worrying about and preparing our daughters for the minuscule threat of stranger danger than we do for the more likely threat of eating disorders.

Poor body image affects quality of life

Your daughter's body image is one of the biggest factors that will determine whether or not she likes herself and if she will live a good life. In severe cases, body image could mean the difference between life and death. But your daughter doesn't need to develop an eating disorder to be seriously affected by a poor body image. A poor body image can influence every aspect of your daughter's life: her mental health, her physical health, her self-esteem, her relationships, her professional ambition, and even her finances.

The amount of money that many young women feel they need to spend on beauty treatments just to be considered acceptable has the potential to keep them poor. Finance expert Pete Wargent calculated that what young women spend on 'basic beauty services' equates to $14,000 a year. 'Let's say you invested that money in the stock market and achieved net returns of about 7 to 8 per cent over time,' says Wargent, the author of *Wealth Ways for the Young: What the rich are teaching their kids about money today*. 'That could see you with a balance rapidly swelling towards $250,000 over about a decade.' Even if the young women put the money they would normally spend on fake eyelashes, spray tans, laser and injectables into a term deposit, they could have a six-figure nest egg in about six years, says Wargent.[4] This figure does not even include beauty products such as make-up and serums. It also doesn't include the cost of cosmetic surgery, where women's body hatred drives them to quite literally risk their lives with non-essential medical procedures.

Younger girls are increasingly concerned about their bodies. Among young Australians, concern about body image is one of the top four issues kids worry about. (The other three concerns are: coping with stress; school or study problems; and mental health.[5]) A poor body image is a precursor to serious social, medical and mental health issues including anxiety, depression, social with-drawal, and social disapproval.[6]

And poor body image is no longer just a concern of tweens and teens. Girls as young as five report worrying about their weight and appearance.[7] Three mothers have told us of their daughters saying that they'd like to get a knife and slice off part of their stomach. All of these girls are under ten and yet they want to slice themselves like a Christmas ham. It's heartbreaking that among their thoughts about fairies and gel pens is an intolerable hatred of their young bodies.

Skinny and pretty are no protection

If your daughter is thin and pretty you may be tempted to skip this chapter. Many of us fall for the idea that if we were thin and pretty enough, life would be perfect. If your daughter's weight falls within the range deemed to be 'thin', you might assume that her body image is just fine. And you may well be right.

But being thin and pretty does not guarantee immunity from poor body image. That's partly because of the effect of media influence – both the Instagram and the telly kinds – but the bigger reason that the shape and size of your daughter's body won't protect her is that body confidence isn't about how she looks. It's based on how she *feels* about how she looks.

You just have to listen to any supermodel list her 'flaws' and read about their obsessive weight-loss regimes to realise that thin and pretty doesn't guarantee body confidence. Even Heidi Klum, who made a career as a Victoria's Secret underwear model, laments her 'pear shape'. She's not the only uber-thin, tall, beautiful woman to have bad body thoughts. Cindy Crawford was quoted as saying, 'Oh god, I have to be so brave,' when she was doing a swimsuit photo shoot. 'See,' she exclaimed, 'every woman hates herself from behind.'[8] This was from a woman who has her own series of fitness videos and was ranked number five on *Playboy*'s list of the '100 Sexiest Stars of the Century' and is on many other 'most beautiful' lists. Despite having a CV straight from a teenage boy's bedroom wall, Cindy Crawford has spent her life feeling her body was not good enough.

We all know of classically beautiful women who are obsessed with losing the last five kilograms as if their life depended on it. There are countless examples of skinny girls and women who are consumed and crushed by body hatred, disordered eating and addictions to exercise and cosmetic surgery. We all also know women whose bodies fall outside the current standards of beauty who have reasonably good body images. What's important is their perceptions of their body – and the importance they place on that perception. Being thin does not guarantee that your daughter will like her body or herself.

There can be two girls who look very similar, and one will be crippled by a hatred of her body, and all the insecurities that go along with it, while the other girl will go through life blissfully unworried by concerns about her body. That's because when it comes to body confidence, how girls think and feel about their bodies is way more important than how they actually look.

Body confidence will not make your daughter 'let herself go'

Whenever a conversation with other parents turns to body confidence, one concern that often comes up is that this whole body confidence thing might 'go too far'. While many parents are fine with the idea of encouraging their daughter to have body confidence in principle, they don't want her to feel *too* comfortable about her body.

Their reasoning seems to be that if their daughter becomes too comfortable in her own skin, she'll 'let herself go' and get fat and therefore unhealthy. Because we equate being thin with happiness, and being fat with unhappiness, these parents are worried that too much body confidence could be setting their daughter up for a life of unhappiness.

Therefore, they conclude that it is their job as parents to manage their daughter's body and appetite until she is old enough to police herself. The reasoning is that if they make their daughter aware of her flaws, and instil in her a fear of becoming fat, then she will develop body vigilance and stay thin, which will allow her to lead a happy life.

Policing your daughter's appetite and body size won't end well

The problem with this way of thinking is that it doesn't work. There is no evidence to suggest that having a positive body image leads people to get fat. Meanwhile, there is plenty of research that shows that having a poor body image isn't conducive to happiness or health – and it may even lead to weight gain. For example, a 2018 study published in the journal *BMC Medicine* found that stigma around weight led to weight gain for those who were the target of the stigma. People who are shamed or ridiculed about their weight are less likely to engage in exercise.[9] That makes intuitive sense; after all, if you don't like your body, then what are the chances you're going to look after it?

But the more surprising – and disturbing – finding from this study is that people who are stigmatised for their weight are also likely to experience a range of other changes in their bodies that make losing weight more difficult, such as increased cortisol levels.

Our bodies release cortisol when we are stressed, and increased cortisol levels in the body promote weight gain.

Dr Rick Kausman, author of *If Not Dieting, Then What?*, has over twenty-five years' experience running a weight management and eating behaviour clinic and is a fellow of the Australian Society for Psychological Medicine. He says that it is absurd to think that we would look after something we are taught to hate.

'Imagine if our body was a car. What would you do to a car you loathed and didn't value or respect? You'd run it into the ground, you wouldn't bother getting it serviced regularly, you'd hardly ever wash it,' says Dr Kausman. 'Now think about a car that you valued. Think of how much more time and effort you would devote to caring for it.'

The bottom line is that girls do not need their parents to focus on their body weight. There is a A$300 billion global weight-loss industry out there that will do it for them.[10] If endlessly pointing out body flaws was the path to thinness then it's likely everyone would be thin – and therefore happy and secure – and these industries wouldn't be the bloated behemoths they are.

Making a point of what and how much your daughter puts in her mouth sends the message that she must be constantly at war with her appetite and the natural state of her body. It inadvertently teaches her to distrust her innate self. And if she ends up distrusting her body then she is less likely to want to look after it.

What our girls need to hear from their parents, more than anything, is that regardless of a world that tells them that their bodies are flawed, they are good enough just the way they are. Our girls need us to be on their team, not Team Weight Loss or Team Beauty Industry.

Body confidence is not the same as body love

Before we get to strategies to instil body confidence, let's get something out of the way up front: your daughter does not have to

LOVE her body to have body confidence. In fact, it may even be better if she doesn't.

This might seem odd given the 'love your body' campaigns that girls and women have been bombarded with over recent years. You know the ones. They're usually sponsored by cosmetics companies and show women stripping down to their bra and undies. They always come with uplifting messages and hashtags about loving the skin you're in.

Body-love campaigns may (slightly) broaden the definition of what is beautiful but they still tell girls and women that they should spend their time and energy focusing on their bodies. In doing so, they reinforce the idea that girls' and women's appearance is what defines their worth – and that's probably not surprising, given that these campaigns are often sponsored by cosmetics companies. After all, it's easier to sell cosmetics, soaps and creams to those who are obsessed with how they look.

But while girls and women are busy 'loving' their bodies, they are not thinking about other activities, relationships and endeavours that can potentially bring real happiness and meaning in life. Rather than dreaming about making a difference in the world, our young women set their sights on perfecting their bikini bodies, with 25 per cent of women aged between 18 and 35 claiming they would rather win *America's Next Top Model* than a Nobel Peace Prize.[11]

The only way to win in the beauty game is to not play

Another well-meaning but potentially counterproductive strategy parents often use to build up their daughter's body confidence is to tell them they are beautiful. If you constantly tell your daughter that she's pretty and beautiful from an early and impressionable age, she will simply believe it and have body confidence. That's the theory, anyhow. But the opposite may be true in practice.

As with the idea of body love, if people are always talking about how pretty a girl is then the girl will naturally assume that her beauty is really important. In fact, talk about it often enough and she may start thinking that it's her most interesting and significant quality.

Dr Renee Engeln, psychologist and author of *Beauty Sick*, says, 'Every time we talk about how a girl or woman looks, we send the message that looks are what's important. When we praise girls for looking pretty, what they can hear is, "I'm of value to others only when I look a certain way."'[12]

Not only that, but by attaching such meaning to external beauty standards we're also sending our girls the message that what other people think about their bodies is more important – much more important – than what they think about themselves. As Sarah McMahon, a psychologist and eating disorder specialist, says, 'Beauty is, after all, a judgement bestowed upon us by other people – and it can be taken away just as quickly. If a girl's sense of identity is based on beauty, it is at the mercy of other people and not herself.'

Placing so much importance on beauty can set our girls up for failure because, no matter how beautiful your daughter is, in our culture it is not possible for any girl or woman to ever be beautiful enough (just ask Cindy Crawford!). Due to the combined forces of Photoshop, Instagram and the beauty, diet and cosmetic surgery industries, what counts as beautiful is constantly shifting. Everyone fails in some way.

It may sound counterintuitive but one of the best ways you can build your daughter's body confidence is to simply stop talking about how beautiful she is.

What is true body confidence?

When we talk about body confidence, we are not talking about your daughter strutting her stuff in a bikini or posing for selfies.

Body confidence is about our daughters trusting their bodies to do all they need to do so they can live the life they want. It's about our daughters liking and respecting their bodies enough to want to care for them, and not allowing negative influences and feelings about their bodies to get in the way of living their lives.

The key to your daughter's body confidence is not for her to be beautiful or even for her to *believe* she is beautiful. It's about not caring that much whether or not she is 'beautiful'.

What really matters in determining your daughter's body confidence is how much she cares about her 'beauty'. How much does her perception of her appearance influence her self-worth? Rather than putting our efforts into making our girls believe they are beautiful – against all odds – we need to shift their focus so that it's not something they dwell on and obsess over.

If instilling your daughter with body confidence sounds impossible, think about how little girls behave. Very young girls have no sense of beauty, they don't view themselves as an object to be looked at, appraised and admired by other people. Their body exists for them, and they have no concept of how pleasing it is or isn't to other people. They are far more concerned about whether their body can run fast or climb.

It is adults who make girls believe that their beauty is the most important thing about them. Our aim is to inoculate our girls against these toxic messages as best we can, so that they spend as little time thinking about their beauty as possible. We want them to define and value themselves for their character, their kindness, their creativity and their bravery. When they wish for different physical characteristics, which is probably inevitable, we want it to be fleeting. When they dress up and adorn themselves, we want them to do it for their own reasons – because it's fun and creative – not because they are trying to meet someone else's standard of beauty and acceptability.

There is no doubt that we have a massive fight on our hands to reduce the importance of physical beauty in our girls' lives. Girls receive countless messages every day from the media, friends, family and even strangers, telling them that being beautiful is important above all else. Many girls grow up believing that they owe the world their beauty and if they fail to be beautiful they are worthless.

But here's the thing: we can choose to be part of the problem by reinforcing this damaging belief, or we can be part of the solution by doing everything we can to protect our girls from a culture of beauty that encourages self-loathing and insecurity. That battle is constant and the forces confronting you can come from unexpected quarters – even Santa Claus.

Sometimes, even Santa gets it wrong

We were in a department store for our annual family Christmas photo. Violet, who was four at the time, had just ridden on Santa's express train and was excited to see the big man in red. We were led by a smiley elf (read: underpaid drama graduate) into Santa's little house.

And then things got weird.

Santa proceeded to comment on every item of clothing Violet was wearing – including her socks. He then told her she was the most beautiful and best-dressed person in the department store. He could have just left it at that. But no, the jolly red bloke ploughed on to suggest our preschooler should be a model when she grows up.

Comparing notes with a friend who took her four-year-old son to the same Santa's grotto, we discovered that Santa hadn't focused on the boy's appearance to break the ice. Instead, he had talked to the boy about Rudolph the Red-Nosed Reindeer. Now, Violet's enthusiasm for Rudolph was as keen as any boy's. In fact, she loved the entire pack. Santa could have bonded with Violet over their mutual regard for flying reindeer. He could have even talked about boring old non-flying deer. Violet would have been thrilled.

But, no, Santa's only interest in Violet was a) her prettiness, b) her comparative prettiness to other girls and women in the store and c) whether she was interested in making a career out of being judged by, and valued for, her looks.

We speak to boys like people and girls like dolls

We know we're being tough on Santa. The jolly old guy meant well. And if telling girls that the only thing about them worth discussing is their looks was a once-a-year event, like Christmas, then Santa's comments wouldn't matter much.

But people focus on girls' appearances all year round. Nearly every time girls leave the house they hear 'That's a pretty dress' or 'What lovely hair you have' or 'You have the most amazing eyelashes' or 'I like the bows on your shoes' or 'You are so cute'.

These daily messages to girls about their appearance are made by well-intentioned, lovely people who, without even realising it, treat boys like people and girls like dolls.

We're not suggesting that people should never remark on girls' appearance. The problem occurs when appearance-related comments make up the majority of what girls hear about themselves. Think for a moment about all the comments that have ever been directed to your daughter over the course of her life – from a newborn to now. We're betting that if you recorded them all and counted them up, she has received more comments about her appearance than all the other comments combined.

If family, friends, teachers, shop assistants, complete strangers, and even Santa only remark on how girls look, rather than what they think and do, how can we expect girls to believe that they have anything other than their beauty to offer the world? Similarly, how can we expect them to be anything other than crushed when they realise they are not as beautiful as the world says they should be? It's hard to like yourself when you realise you do not measure up to the only thing about you that you have been told matters.

How to speak to girls

We are just as guilty as everybody else when it comes to remarking on girls' appearance. The first thought that rushes into our heads when we see our girls and other little girls is how cute and adorable they are. The focus on girls' appearance to the exclusion of almost everything else is so deeply entrenched that many of us often don't know what else to say to them. Despite our best intentions, many of us have no experience of engaging with girls on any level other than the superficial.

Yet little boys are gorgeous too, and that's not the first or only thing we ever say to them. We figure if we can treat boys as people instead of dolls then, with some thought and practice, we can treat girls the same way. If you're stuck, here's a list of suggestions for ice-breakers/conversation starters with girls:

- Where have you been today? or Where are you going today?
- How old are you?
- What do you want to be when you grow up?
- What's your favourite book/toy/sport/animal/food/song?
- Do you know any Christmas carols?
- What did you have for lunch?
- Did you have a good sleep last night?
- Check out your surroundings and remark on something such as a flowering plant, a truck, a picture on the wall, even the weather.

Comment on or ask a question about what the girl is doing at that moment, such as 'You were running fast just then' or 'That's a big tower you're building' or 'What's your toy dog's name?'

If none of these is appropriate or works, you can just imagine what you would say to a boy in the same situation. Chances are it will be equally suitable.

DRM: Diluting, redirecting and modelling

We would love to say that we have the guts to shut down all the appearance-based comments people make to our girls. The truth is, we find this really hard, especially since we know that people mean well. It would be awkward, tedious and rude to challenge appearance-related compliments every time they occurred, but we still don't want our girls hearing them. Our solution is to dilute and redirect these comments, so that every time our girls hear something about their appearance they also hear something else about themselves as a counterbalance. We also model other ways to engage with girls and women without discussing their appearance.

1. Dilution

With dilution, we point out other qualities our daughters possess that aren't related to appearance. For example, if our neighbour says that our girls are growing more beautiful every day, we'll mention other traits that are also growing, such as their reading ability, their cartwheeling prowess, and their persistence, humour and kindness.

2. Redirection

Redirection is also known as changing the subject. For example, a comment on our girls' clothes can be expanded to thinking about what they can do and achieve in those clothes. 'Your dress is very pretty,' for example, becomes an opportunity to highlight that it's good for climbing trees in. A comment about a jumper can be redirected into a conversation about the weather, such as 'We need to keep warm because we're going to play at the park.'

The more a redirection highlights our girls' capacity to act – what they can do – the better. We don't want them to think that they are just passive objects to be admired.

3. Modelling

We rarely discuss our girls' appearance in front of them. Occasionally we will remark on their beauty because we wouldn't want them to think that we are silent on the topic because we don't think they are beautiful. But we limit our comments about their appearance because we want them to know that how they look is not important to us. We also want them to know that how other people look is just as unimportant. As such, we do not make appearance-based comments about anybody – good or bad – in front of our girls. Appearance is just not a topic we discuss. Remember, it's not just negative comments about your daughters' or other people's bodies that are harmful. As weight-management psychologist Glenn Mackintosh writes in *Thinsanity*, '[T]oo much talk – of any kind – about bodies, looks and appearance can eat away at body acceptance.'[13]

Rethinking weight

The issues surrounding weight and fat are complicated and, despite what you see on Instagram or hear about the latest fad diet, science does not have the answers. Sixty years of failed public health campaigns and diet culture have taught us one lesson: weight and weight loss are not simple matters of willpower or calories in versus calories out.

If diets worked, we'd all be thin and the diet industry would have collapsed a long time ago. We now know that even if everyone ate the same food and did the same amount of exercise each day, there would still be an enormous range in people's body size, shape and weight.[14] We also know that you can't judge a person's health just by looking at their body. Thin people can be terribly unhealthy, and it is also possible – and common – for people with larger bodies to be healthy, happy and live long lives.[15]

Your daughter's health is not derived from the size and shape of her body. Nor is it about the number on the scales or her Body Mass Index (BMI), which was a set of numbers made up by a mathematician – not a health professional – and was never intended to be a measure of individual health. And having a body that is bigger than the fashion industry says it should be does not mean that your daughter will dislike herself. As one girl said to us, 'I wish they'd make jeans that actually fit.' In her mind, the problem of her ill-fitting jeans resided totally with their manufacturer and not her curvy body.

Forget about weight

Whenever we write or speak about the dangers of focusing on weight and weight-loss dieting, we inevitably get accused of promoting obesity and unhealthy lifestyles. This could not be further from the truth. We want our girls to be healthy. We know that good health will aid our girls in liking themselves and living the lives they want. But let's be clear that an obsessive focus on weight and weight loss is not going to deliver good health.

Dr Kausman says that when it comes to health, people have been focusing on the wrong 'w'. The key to health is not 'weight', it's 'wellness'. Weight is an outcome, a number on the scale, whereas wellness is a process. Wellness is about living a healthy, balanced lifestyle. It's about eating well most of the time, moving our bodies in enjoyable ways, and engaging with life in ways that make us happy.

We absolutely do care about the food our daughters eat and the exercise they do, and we will go into more detail about this later in the chapter. But just like beauty, our goal is to do everything we can to reduce the importance of body *weight* in our girls' lives. If we want our girls to live in ways that are fun, healthy and active, they must focus on what their bodies can *do* rather than how they appear. Your daughter is unlikely to like herself if she is obsessed with counting calories, depriving her body, and feeling ashamed when her attempts at weight-loss dieting inevitably fail.

While many parents are happy to get on board with girls possessing body confidence, it often comes with one condition: just as long as she's already thin. What's left unsaid here is that if your daughter isn't thin, then she doesn't get to feel good about herself.

'But if my daughter is fat, isn't it my job to tell her?'

That's the question one dad asked us after reading an article about children and body image. It wasn't the first time we'd been asked a question like this, although parents usually aren't so direct.

To be clear, this dad cared about his daughter's health. He'd heard all the horror stories about childhood obesity and figured that if he didn't tell his daughter to lose a few pounds then he was probably failing in his job at being a father. But the dad was also wondering if he was doing the right thing in taking a body-shaming approach.

He was right to have second thoughts.

While we don't know his daughter, it's more than likely that she already knows about her weight. The list of people who have possibly beaten this dad to this particular weight conversation include:

- frenemies
- school bullies
- medical professionals
- the aunt who gasps audibly when his daughter asks for a second piece of birthday cake
- complete strangers who raise their eyebrows every time she eats in public
- every second TV show, magazine, newspaper or movie.

It's highly likely that nobody judges this girl's body more harshly than she does herself. But don't take it from us. Dr Kausman's expert advice is this: nothing good can come from focusing on weight. Not your child's weight, not your weight, not anyone's weight.

'The research is quite clear that focusing on weight does not result in weight loss,' says Dr Kausman. 'In fact, it will most likely result in weight gain. It's also the most common pathway to an eating disorder, particularly with kids.'

Psychologist Sarah McMahon agrees, saying that girls who already feel vulnerable and exposed will only feel worse if put on a weight-loss diet. 'Parents putting their kids on a weight-loss diet has social implications too,' says McMahon. 'It ostracises them from their friends, prevents them from engaging in social events; it sends a message that there is something wrong with them that needs to be fixed.'

The message that your daughter could get from this approach is that you will love her more if she's thinner. What she really needs is for her home to be a safe haven, a place where she feels loved, valued and respected no matter what.

Dr Katja Rowell, a US doctor and an expert in childhood eating problems, says that although there is a lot of concern about childhood obesity we should not ignore the very real risks from putting children on diets. 'We know from our best quality evidence that weight lost through diets is regained virtually across the board,' says Dr Rowell, who is the author of *Helping Your Child with Extreme Picky Eating*. 'Dieting in children is linked to increased depression, and is a major risk factor for the development of eating disorders, which are costly and involve incredible suffering.'

If you're still undecided about telling your daughter to lose weight, consider this: you're asking her to do something that the vast majority of adults are unable to do. As a 2015 study of 99,791 obese women and 76,704 obese men found, 'The annual probability of patients with simple obesity attaining a normal body weight was only 1 in 124 for women and 1 in 210 for men.'[16] That is the definition of setting your child up for a lifetime of failure and shame.

Dietitian and body-image advocate Meg McClintock says even positive comments about someone's body or weight loss can lead to a destructive focus on body shape and size. 'It creates weight stigma and bias and if children aren't fitting into the thin ideal, or don't think they are, then they internalise the negative stereotypes,' she says. 'This increases their chances of depression, lowers their self-acceptance and reduces satisfaction with life in general.'

This is our reply to the father who wondered if he should tell his daughter that she is fat: what a girl really needs from her parents – particularly her father, since he's the first man who loves her and sets the standard for the way she'll expect men to treat her in the future – is not shame and judgement, but unconditional love and a safe space to grow up.

What if you think your daughter is above her natural body weight?

When we talk about natural body weight, we are not referring to the BMI. Your daughter's natural body weight is whatever it happens to be when she is living a healthy and active life.

If you think your daughter is above her natural body weight, the first step is to forget about appearance. While we're often quick to judge people based on appearance, it turns out that it's a poor indicator of health. 'Even though you might think that your daughter is a higher weight than her peers, there is no way of telling just by looking at her if she is above her most healthy weight,' says Dr Kausman.

Instead of trying to change your daughter's weight, shift your focus to wellness. Look at her behaviour and see if there are changes that can be made to become healthier. If the goal is weight loss, then it's most likely your daughter will fail at it every day, which will crush her self-esteem and happiness. But if the goal is living a healthy lifestyle, such as eating well most of the time and being active, then that's an area where she can have control and succeed.

This may be hard to accept, given that we grew up believing that getting the body you want is a simple matter of willpower. But if your daughter's behaviour around food and exercise is normal then she is probably at her natural body weight. She is already how she is supposed to be.

Sarah McMahon says that bodies really do come in different shapes and sizes. Rather than fighting what will most likely be a losing battle, trying to turn your daughter's body into something it was never meant to be, work out how to support your daughter in approaching life in a body that may not meet our current beauty ideal. 'Help your daughter to realise that thinness doesn't bring happiness. She doesn't need to be thin for her life to start. Life is happening right now,' says McMahon.

Once we reject the lie that thinness is the path to happiness, our daughters can direct their energy and attention towards finding activities that will bring them the joy and the acceptance they are seeking.

How to help your daughter accept her body

One of the best explanations we have ever seen to help children (and their parents) accept their bodies, even if they differ from the thin ideal, comes from Glenn Mackintosh in his book *Thinsanity*:

This may sound weird, so bear with me, but one way I think about us is being like dogs in the dog park. That's right: we are all dogs in the dog park. Now, some of us are pretty little toy poodles. And that's great! But we run into trouble if all the dogs start to become unhappy because they're not toy poodles. Because some of them are labradors, some are greyhounds and some are mastiffs. A mastiff will never become a poodle, no matter how hard she tries. If she goes on a weight loss kick she'll never reach toy poodle weight, and anything she loses she'll gain back, as *that's what her body is telling her to do.* She's better off being the happiest mastiff she can be, and hoping her owners feed her well enough and provide opportunities to get out and play so she can be the healthiest one too. Luckily for dogs, they don't spend a second worrying about this stuff. Dogs are happy! Which means they're smarter than us. Let's all be a bit more like dogs.

A girl who likes herself is a first-rate mastiff (or whatever breed), not a second-rate poodle.

What if your daughter is teased for being 'fat'?

A friend's daughter recently came home from kinder in tears because another kid had called her fat. She is four years old.

As a parent it's heartbreaking to see your child being teased for being fat, and it's very difficult to know what to say and do. We approached three experts for their advice on how to help girls handle a fat-phobic world.

Sarah McMahon, psychologist and director of BodyMatters Australasia

Do: Take your child's concerns seriously

Check in with your child to find out how they feel about their body. Try to do it in the same way you would make time to discuss any other concerns they have, such as how they're getting on with their friends or their studies. Parents can be powerful agents in building body confidence and body trust. Be mindful of how you talk about your body, their body and other people's bodies. People should never be shamed for their bodies. Ever.

That includes you. Be kinder to yourself. Avoid 'fat chat' or 'diet talk' about your own life and those of others.

Don't: Encourage weight loss or dieting

Encouraging weight loss will serve to validate the opinion of body bullies. It will send the message that yes, your child's body actually is defective, ugly, unhealthy, overweight and cannot be trusted around food.

Avoid dieting yourself. It models and normalises this unhealthy behaviour and can pass on body anxieties to your child. After all, if a child thinks there is something wrong with your body, they might assume there is something wrong with theirs.

Dr Rick Kausman, medical doctor, board member of The Butterfly Foundation and author of *If Not Dieting, Then What?*
Do: Understand that weight and wellness are not the same thing
Contrary to popular belief, you cannot judge a person's health just by looking at them or calculating their BMI. Kids grow at different rates, bodies change over time, and all bodies are different. Instead of worrying about your child's shape and size, put your energies into providing the best environment you can to help your child be as healthy as they can. Focus on the process of living a healthy life, rather than weight loss as a goal.

Don't: Put your child on a diet
Nothing good can come from weight-loss dieting. The research is very clear: if a person focuses on weight and changing weight, it doesn't last. Very often it results in more weight gain.

Don't treat your children differently based on their weight. Don't allow the skinny child to have an extra serve of chocolate while denying the child with a bigger body. Children will rebel against that, sneak food and become 'closet eaters' full of shame around their eating.

Dana Kerford, friendship expert and founder of URSTRONG
Do: Empower your child to stand up to hurtful comments and behaviour
Children who get away with saying hurtful comments will continue to do so. Teaching your child to stand up for themselves also helps to build their sense of self-worth, reinforcing that they don't deserve to be treated unkindly. If your child is the target of hurtful comments, shower them with love, affection and positive affirmations. Remind them how amazing they are and encourage them to spend time with friends who make them feel good.

Don't: Tell your child to 'just ignore them'
If the child who says the hurtful comments receives no consequences for their behaviour, that behaviour is implicitly

reinforced. This makes them likely to engage in the same behaviour again. The reality is that children can't ignore other children who are being mean on purpose. The key to raising resilient, confident children who can face adversity with their heads held high is teaching them to stand up for themselves (more on this on page 162). Remind them to surround themselves with people who treat them with respect, and help them to understand that when someone calls them a name, it says more about the name-caller than it does about them.

Be prepared for pre-puberty weight gain

Many girls gain weight in preparation for puberty. It's what girls' bodies need to do in order to menstruate. It doesn't mean that there's something wrong or that corrective action should be taken.

Instead, a girl needs reassurance from the people who love her that these changes are normal and she should trust her body. But this can be the time when well-meaning family and friends start making comments about your daughter's increased appetite or weight gain. These comments can be incredibly damaging at a time when she may already be sensitive about her changing body.

One sure way to shut down this kind of body shaming at a family lunch is to mention the word puberty. Say something like: '[Daughter's name]'s body is getting ready for puberty. Do you want to have a discussion about fat stores and menstruation or should we just get back to lunch?'

If this is a little too confrontational (or mortifying for your daughter!) then you can always change the subject to the weather or ask someone to pass the salt. Then afterwards you can talk to your daughter about criticism (as we discuss in the Power Perspective chapter) and remind her that some people have earned the right to be listened to, and some people haven't.

Minimise exposure to toxic messages

Girls need to know that many of the images they see of girls and women on social media, magazines, billboards, packaging and even toys are not real.

Use media images to teach your daughter about bodies. For example, have conversations about how unrealistic Barbie's proportions are. Point out that if women's legs really were as long as Barbie's and their waists were that thin, then they wouldn't be able to stand up.

Girls are largely defenceless against a range of negative messages from advertising, which can be detrimental to their body image, lifestyle choices and self-esteem. Don't just take our word for it. Fast Company, which describes itself as 'the world's leading progressive business media brand', let the cat out of the bag when it shared a secret about effective advertising with its readers: 'Induce fear, uncertainty and doubt.'[18] This advertising practice is so well established it's even got its own acronym, FUD.

In a world where childhood anxiety is at a record high, eating disorders are on the rise, and eight-year-old girls are being admitted to hospital suffering from anorexia nervosa, we reckon our children don't need any more FUD in their lives. Awareness and media literacy are important, but they are not enough. The research shows that even knowing that an image has been photoshopped is not enough to stop us from feeling bad about ourselves. To protect our own daughters from these unrealistic standards of beauty, we have minimised their exposure to them. The fewer ads children see the better.

Of course there are some people, such as Adrian Furnham, Professor of Psychology at University College London, who see no problem at all with advertising to children. The *Guardian* reported on Furnham playing the universal Corporate Responsibility Dodging Card. It's called: blaming parents. 'It is not advertising that harms children, but irresponsible parenting,' Furnham wrote in a pamphlet for the Social Affairs Unit, a free-market think tank. 'Children are far more sophisticated consumers than popularly imagined. There is no respectable intellectual argument for the view that advertising alone creates false wants and parental conflicts.'[19]

Sure, there are many factors involved in childhood eating disorders, body-image problems and cultivating anxieties, but advertising is a pretty big one.

If advertising is really all about providing information rather than emotional manipulation, Coke wouldn't spend US$5.8 billion per year on advertising and marketing.[20] It's not like we are unaware of the soft drink's existence. And anyone who thinks children are highly sophisticated consumers of media has obviously never met a child confronted with L.O.L. dolls, Shopkins or a My Little Pony.

That's why we try to make our house an ad-free zone. Gossip and fashion magazines (which wrote the book on inducing body insecurity) are not allowed in our house. Even flyers that advertise beauty treatments and weight-loss products get dumped in the recycling bin between the letterbox and the front door. And, unlike when we were growing up, it's now really easy to keep children away from TV advertising. (Thank you, ABC!)

The ABC's two ad-free children's channels – ABC Kids and ABC Me – are an absolute godsend for parents. When people complain about our taxpayer dollars going to the ABC's kids channels, they are missing the most important point: it's not so much about what's on these channels, but what's *not* on them. FUD-free TV is an investment in the mental health of our next generation.

There are also other ad-free TV options. In our house, we also let our girls watch programs from ad-free streaming services such as iview, Netflix or Stan. Occasionally they can watch programs on YouTube, but you need to be careful about closing the site when the show finishes, given that literally anything is two clicks away.

Don't get us wrong – we let our girls watch as much TV as every other busy parent who thinks they really should be cutting

51

back. But our girls' exposure to the harmful messages of advertising is limited to whatever product-placement producers can pack into the episode itself.

Make sure to also be cautious about what your daughter is seeing on her – or your – social media feeds. These images can be even more toxic because they often appear to be spontaneous and based on real life, even though they are as carefully curated and manipulated as the cover of a glossy magazine.

Meg McClintock cautions parents to be aware of harmful images that masquerade as health messages. 'Thinspiration is not inspiring and is more likely to lead to higher levels of body dissatisfaction, which can lead to doing fewer life-affirming activities such as playing sport and participating actively in class.'

The key to body confidence is trust

Babies are born understanding their own appetites. They know when they're full and when they're hungry. Unless they stop eating and are losing weight, we mostly trust babies to regulate their own appetites. But as babies grow into children, we suddenly decide that their appetites should no longer be trusted. We teach them in so many ways that they should ignore the natural signals their bodies give them about when they are hungry and when they are full, and even worse, that these signals are something to be ashamed of.

Dr Katja Rowell says that as soon as children start eating solids, many parents try to control their daughters' appetites. 'What I see most often is parents trying to get children to eat less,' says Dr Rowell. 'Parents routinely tell me that they worry their infant will be fat, so they try to distract them from eating and leave them crying for more food. This can lead to food-preoccupied toddlers and, in my opinion, is a precursor to binge eating.'

Girls and women, in particular, are bombarded with unsolicited diet advice on a daily basis about what's okay to eat, when it's okay to eat it, what macro-nutrient they should be avoiding this month, and how many calories they should or shouldn't be consuming. All of these messages tell women that their bodies are deceitful enemies that need to be battled with – and contained.

Accredited dietitian Rachel Gerathy says that, just like when they were babies, our girls' bodies know how to regulate their appetites and body weight. Parents should teach girls that their body knows when it is hungry and when it is full, and all they have to do is listen to it.

'We should be encouraging children to listen to their body's internal regulation cues for hunger and satiety, allowing them to consume a range of wholesome foods with varied tastes and textures within the realms of a balanced nutritional intake,' says Gerathy.

That means allowing girls to eat as much as they want. Yes, really. As the Victorian government advises on its Better Health portal, 'Your role as parent of a toddler is to decide what food and when to offer it, but the child decides whether or not to eat and how much they'll eat. Remember that children eat when they're hungry.'[21]

If we can trust babies and toddlers to read their own bodies, we should trust older children to do this too.

This doesn't mean that girls should have free rein to eat chicken nuggets and ice cream all day, every day. Parents can still ensure their girl eats nutritious food by making sure that the food they provide is mostly healthy. But your daughter gets to decide how much of the food she wants to eat. If she wants a second helping of dinner or dessert, the answer should be yes.

This may sound shocking to you, and that's not surprising. For hundreds of years, most boys and men have been allowed to eat as much as they like, but women and girls have been required to restrict and deprive themselves. Many of us grew up in households where women declared proudly, 'I'm only a little eater,' before bingeing when they thought nobody was watching. Whereas boys were allowed an extra slice of cake, a girl who made the same request would be shamed with raised eyebrows or a cutting remark. It makes no sense to think that boys' bodies are able to regulate their appetites but girls' bodies are not.

The message that girls should restrict their eating is still so pervasive it can even be found in books that are supposed to be empowering. For example, when Violet was seven a bookseller recommended a middle-grade series, claiming it had lots of positive messages for young girls. We beg to differ. In this 'empowering' story, a girl has a sleepover at a friend's house. The family has spaghetti bolognese for dinner. The girl likes the spaghetti bolognese so she has a second helping. That night the girl lies in bed in a fit of anxiety, worrying that the family will think she's a pig. The message woven through the pages of this supposed 'girl power' book is that a girl's character can be measured by what she eats and that other people are policing her appetite and judging her accordingly. Of course, the story has a happy ending and the girl's worry is found to be baseless, but the concept of body policing is still presented to young readers as normal.

The rule of 'parents provide, children decide' also applies when girls do not eat as much as adults think they should. Insisting children finish everything that's on their plate is another way of teaching girls to ignore what their body is telling them.

The one food rule that works well at mealtimes in our house is for our girls to eat something of everything on their plates so that their bodies get the variety of nutrients they need to grow and be healthy. Sometimes that means they will only eat one pea or half a bean. Other times, when they are having a growth spurt or have had a particularly active day, they will eat more dinner than us – including vegetables. We've noticed that our girls' appetites vary enormously from one day to the next. And that's okay.

Feeling in control of their own appetite and trusting their body's signals is more important than how much they eat. It also means we avoid any power struggles or battles of will surrounding food.

There are no good and bad foods. There's just food

Have you noticed how food and eating are now moral issues?

People turn down a slice of cake by explaining they're 'being good'. People talk about good and bad foods or good and bad fats. Others talk about 'clean eating', as if other foods – and the people who eat them – are dirty.

Dr Rowell says that some parents think they are teaching healthy eating behaviours when they ban 'unhealthy' or 'bad' foods. In fact, they may be doing the exact opposite. 'When parents strictly avoid all processed foods, sugar, refined flours and refer to those foods as "toxic" or "poison", children really struggle,' says Dr Rowell. 'Food and mealtimes are defined by fear and avoidance. Some children become anxious and more food averse, while others crave and seek out the forbidden foods.'

Fortunately, there is another way: everyday foods, and sometimes foods.

If you want your daughter to develop a healthy relationship with food, try to keep ideas like 'good' and 'bad' far away from discussions of food. Explain to her that she needs to eat a variety of foods every day. Some foods will make her grow, run fast and lift heavy objects. Others will help her to learn, and prevent her from getting sick. And some are just yummy.

Don't prohibit any foods because doing so will create good/bad associations with food. Our own girls understand that they can eat processed foods sometimes because they taste good and they are part of social rituals – like birthday cake, for example – but they don't help their bodies grow. We tell them that if they were to eat too much cake, then they wouldn't be able to fit in all the other foods that their bodies need.

Sarah McMahon recommends parents talk about foods in terms of 'everyday foods' and 'sometimes foods' so that there is no shame or judgement associated with eating. 'If some foods are "bad", and then a child eats them then they will conclude that they are bad too,' McMahon says.

Making children feel ashamed of their appetites and of eating is not only unconducive to raising a girl who likes herself, it may turn your daughter into a closet binge eater. We saw the effects of food shame at a playdate featuring fairy floss for afternoon tea. While the other kids dived in, one little girl declined, saying that she would prefer to eat a carrot instead. She said that carrots are healthy and fairy floss is not. Yes, in isolation carrots are healthier than fairy floss. But going by what was about to happen, there was nothing healthy about the food choices and behaviour of this girl.

After a time the kids who had happily devoured the fairy floss decided they wanted to go and play. The child who'd said she preferred carrots to concentrated sugar, meanwhile, lingered at the table and, when she thought nobody was looking, stuffed her face with fairy floss. The fairy floss was left on the table and throughout the course of the afternoon we watched the girl sneak more mouthfuls of it. This child not only ended up eating quite a lot of fairy floss, she also suffered from the embarrassment of wanting to eat it, and the shame of not having enough willpower to resist it. It is asking a lot to expect a child to say no to sweet treats that are right in front of them. To the other kids, the fairy floss was just food. To this child, it was a test of her moral character – a test she might have felt she failed.

If no food is off limits, though, how do we stop our girls from wanting lollies and cake for dinner every night?

Following the rule of 'parents provide, children decide', we mostly have only 'everyday food' in our house so when our girls decide what to eat, they are usually selecting from healthy and nutritious foods.

Food and emotions

There are times when girls want to eat even though they are clearly not hungry. When your daughter asks for food and you suspect that she is not hungry, ask her to check in with her body to see if she is hungry or if she is just bored. If she says she is hungry, trust her and offer her as much 'everyday food' as she wants. If she is bored, then ask her about what else she might like to do.

If your daughter is not hungry and not bored, then there may be something else going on. Ask her if there is a different problem and, if there is, see if you can help her to solve this problem in another way. If she is sad or stressed, for example, then it's better to have a cuddle, or talk about what's bothering her.

This approach makes it clear to girls that they are in charge of their bodies and their appetites. It also demonstrates to your daughter that you trust her to make the right decisions, building trust between you both. This also avoids conflict about food and stand-offs over eating, which just raise the emotional temperature of food. The only emotion you want to instil in your girls around food is pleasure at the feeling that they are in control.

If our girls are having a rough time, we don't use food to cheer them up (such as 'You had a bad day at school? Have an ice cream'). If they're hurt we don't distract them from their pain by giving them a biscuit. We encourage our girls to express their feelings, rather than eating them, and to find more productive ways of dealing with them.

We also try not to use food to manage our girls' behaviour – and we don't always get this right. There have been times when we've been on a phone conference for work and the only way to keep our girls quiet was to put a bag of lollies in front of them. And there were many times when they were babies that we gave them food to keep them in the pram. Sometimes you do whatever works. But in general, we try not to give food as a reward or withhold it as a punishment. Using food to manage behaviour adds an emotional element to food that doesn't need to be there. We want our girls to think of food as just food.

Escaping diet culture

Encouraging a healthy relationship with food also requires us to end our fixation on diet culture. What do we mean by diet culture? Culture is the shorthand way of saying 'how we do things around here'. It's the accepted way of behaving, doing what everyone else does.

Diet culture means, obviously, going on diet after diet after diet as a normal part of life. It's about constantly trying to be smaller than you are. But it is also so much more than that. It means talking about restrictive eating as a regular part of conversation. It's using discussions of weight and appearance and obsessing over food choices to connect with other people (fat chat, as discussed on page 26). It's about using food choices and body shape to judge people's character – your own character and that of other people.

If your daughter is engaging in body talk, explain that people come in all different shapes and sizes and you can't tell by looking at a person if they are healthy or not.

To escape diet culture, and to spare your daughter from diet culture, try not to diet yourself. For many people, though, not dieting is unthinkable. If this is impossible for you, at least try to avoid talking about dieting and weight loss in front of your daughter. Young ears are very impressionable. If you must diet, dietitian Meg McClintock suggests finding other ways to talk about your food choices. 'For example, if you're not having any carbs at dinner don't tell your kids that carbs are bad or that they make you fat,' she suggests. 'Say, "I've had enough of that food group today and I don't need any more."'

Taryn Brumfitt, Australian body-image advocate, writer and director of the 2016 film *Embrace*, says that when a negative comment about our body pops into our heads, we should verbalise it as a positive. For example, 'I hate my tuckshop arms' can be replaced with 'I am grateful for my arms that hug my loved ones.' Or, 'I hate my cellulite and stretch marks on my legs' can be replaced with 'These legs enable me to run, walk, dance and get anywhere I want to go!'

Exercise is supposed to be fun

Exercise is often presented to women as punishment. It's to burn off the extra calories they ate at a party or to fix their flaws in time for summer.

Not only is this approach unlikely to make your daughter a fan of exercise, it's also a quick way to make her hate her body. It's part of seeing her body as an enemy that must be defeated, rather than something to be nurtured.

Encourage your daughter to exercise because it's fun. Nutritionist Justyna Kalka says children need to understand that their bodies are amazing machines and chemical factories, and there can be serious consequences when they try to force their bodies into submission with extreme exercise measures. 'Be an active family, teach your child about the great health benefits of movement, tell them how it strengthens the body healthily,' she says. 'So when they feel vulnerable about their size or shape, they will be more likely to resort to a walk on the beach rather than a week on a diet or some crazy detox they picked up from a magazine.'

Tell your daughter that exercise is essential for the health and function of her body and her brain. But avoid framing that discussion in terms of body shape or appearance. There are so many different ways for children to move their bodies. If your daughter says she hates exercise, then maybe she just hasn't found the right type of exercise for her yet.

If we encourage our kids to be active, to play outside and to eat healthy food because it's good for their growing bodies, bones and brains, and not because they need to hit some arbitrary figure on a weight chart, then we have done our job. More than ever, we need to be teaching our girls that the goal should be the process of living a healthy life and not the outcome of meeting a commercially driven standard of beauty.

Body confidence family health check

The following is a checklist to identify factors that can help or hinder body confidence. It's not a test but it may prompt some conversations with the adults in your family to ensure that your home is a safe haven for your daughter and her developing body confidence.

Protective factors

1. Do you focus on what bodies do rather than how they appear?
2. Do you talk about food in morally neutral language (such as 'everyday foods' and 'sometimes foods')?
3. Do you model exercise as something you do regularly because it's fun and you want to take care of your body?
4. Do you teach your daughter to trust her body and to listen when her body tells her that she's hungry or that she's full?
5. Do you talk to your daughter about the negative and unrealistic portrayals of women and women's bodies in the media and our culture more broadly?
6. Do you protect your daughter from people who will police her body, or do you stand up for her when it happens?
7. Do you refrain from 'fat chat' with your friends in front of your daughter?
8. Do you make an effort to talk about how people are different and that we come in all sorts of colours, shapes and sizes? We all have different qualities and talents.

9. Do you try to keep the negative thoughts you have about your own body to yourself?

10. Do you seek out books, magazines and TV shows that focus on and celebrate what girls do rather than how they appear?

Risk factors

1. Are you on a weight-loss diet?

2. Is your child on a weight-loss diet?

3. Do you talk negatively about your own body size and shape?

4. Do you talk negatively about the appearance of other people's bodies, such as 'She's porked up' or 'She's let herself go' or 'She's aged'?

5. Do you give compliments about people's weight, such as 'You look gorgeous, have you lost weight?'

6. Do you remark on your daughter's appearance first, and more frequently, than any of her other qualities or achievements? For example, at a ballet concert are you more likely to tell her she looked beautiful rather than that she danced well or remembered the steps?

7. Do you remark on or shame your daughter if you think she is eating more than she should? Do you call her 'greedy' or 'piggish', or caution her about getting fat?

8. Do you force your daughter to finish all the food on her plate?

9. Do you police or comment on your daughter's appetite, exercise or physical appearance more than you would if she were a boy?

10. Do you use food as a reward or a punishment (such as 'If you clean your room you will get a lolly')?

11. Do you use food to help your daughter regulate her emotions (such as 'Don't cry, have a cookie')?

12. Do you talk about food using moral language, or label food as 'good' or 'bad'?

13. Do you talk about food in terms of calories and what's fattening and what's not?
14. Do you talk about exercise in negative terms, as a punishment for overindulging or as something you must do to correct a wrong body?
15. Do you tease or give your daughter nicknames that relate to her physical appearance, such as 'chubby', 'skinny mini', 'big ears', 'long legs' or 'carrot top'?
16. Do you consume media in your house that convey negative messages about women's bodies (such as fashion magazines, TV shows like *The Biggest Loser*, or diet books)?

Action for dads

Don't talk about your daughter's body solely in terms of appearance (or about the appearance of anyone else's body in your daughter's presence).

While body-image pressures are rapidly becoming a problem for boys as well as girls, many dads were lucky to grow up in a time when they didn't have to deal with the expectation that they should have a set of six-pack abs. As a result, dads can be blissfully ignorant about their daughter's growing insecurity about her body and do not realise just how damaging their throwaway comments can be.

Psychologist Sarah McMahon says that dads need to be particularly careful about the comments they make about other people's bodies. 'I've heard many examples of dads having an ongoing commentary about other women being attractive,' she says. 'Of course it is really uncomfortable for kids to hear their dads commenting on the attractiveness of women who aren't their mums. But also, talking about people who shouldn't be eating certain foods because they're "too fat" or making moral judgements about people's eating and body shape can be very damaging.'

What NOT to say

With the help of McMahon, we've gathered a list of real examples of damaging body comments girls have reported their dads as saying.

'Look at those legs'
This was said when commenting on the chubby legs of a toddler. It may have been meant as a compliment; however, a girl might internalise the message that her legs are fat and she may hold this belief into her adulthood.

'Fatman'
This was a nickname given to a little girl whose brother loves Batman. Labelling someone or giving a name based on physical attributes, particularly their size, suggests a moral association and leads a child to see themselves entirely as that physical description.

'She's a pretty waitress'
This was a conversation between a dad and a grandfather. It sends the message that appearance matters, attractiveness is rewarded and that policing and surveillance of other people's appearance is normal behaviour.

'You look like a refugee/AIDS patient/cancer patient'
This comment was made to a girl who had lost weight. Aside from the fact that these comments are xenophobic and ableist, they can also be damaging to a girl's body image. Just as we need to be careful about fat-shaming, it is important we don't thin-shame. If someone is naturally thin, they shouldn't be reprimanded for it; if someone has lost weight, criticising them for it is never going to be helpful, particularly if the weight loss has occurred due to problematic behaviour such as disordered eating.

'You'd be a pretty girl if you only lost some weight'
A comment like this implies that a girl cannot be pretty without being thin and perpetuates the idea that being attractive is the most important thing a girl can be.

Aside from avoiding comments that may hinder their daughter's ability to develop body confidence, dads can have a positive influence on their daughter's body confidence. Quality time together and sharing a common interest with your daughter helps her to develop a sense of self that has nothing to do with how she looks. Through your relationship with your daughter's mother, you can also show that women are valued for qualities other than their physical appearance.

Recap

- Constantly telling your daughter she is beautiful is unlikely to build her body confidence. In fact, it's likely to be self-defeating, making her think that her beauty is her most important quality. When she inevitably feels like she doesn't measure up, she will feel worthless.
- The key to your daughter's body confidence is reducing how much she cares about whether or not she's seen as 'beautiful'.
- Don't talk about the appearance of your daughter's body, your body or anyone else's body. The more your daughter values bodies for what they do rather than how they appear, the more likely she is to develop body confidence.
- Girls do not need their parents to point out all their physical 'imperfections' because the whole world has already beaten them to it. What they need to hear from their parents, more than anything, is that they are good enough just the way they are. Our girls need us to be on their team and not Team Beauty or Team Weight Loss.

3

A girl who likes herself owns her body

It's not often that our family has something in common with the Kardashian West clan. But it does happen. Okay, it happened once. It was the time when Kim Kardashian West posted a picture on her Instagram of her five-year-old daughter North wearing – wait for it – lipstick.

That sound you're hearing right now? That's the echo of the combined fury and outrage of the internet breaking loose. One Instagrammer took it upon herself to tell Kim that she is a terrible mother. 'It amazes me that you canot [sic] see what a terribly bad mother you are,' the outraged Instagrammer wrote. 'My child is 6 and has never NEVER asked to wear make-up because she still her inocents [sic]. You gave [sic] ruined your daughter.'

And it wasn't just the lipstick that had people hurling cyber stones. The colour of North's lipstick compounded Kim's crimes against motherhood. You see, the lipstick in question was red. And, as we all know, red is the colour of lust, Communism and the devil. The fact that it's also the colour of Elmo, Santa and the Wiggles' car – not to mention an actual Wiggle – was overlooked on this occasion.

How does this relate to us?

That very same Christmas, in 2018, our girls – then aged nine and four – announced that they wanted to spend their Christmas money on make-up kits. These kits came complete with blushes, bronzers and eyeshadows in around 80 bazillion different shades. And yes, they also included lipsticks. Some were even shades of red.

When our girls made their announcement, our first thought was, 'No bloody way.' We consulted our mental Parenting Rule Book about what age was socially acceptable for girls to wear make-up and concluded that, whatever it was, four and nine was a stretch. We imagined the disapproving looks as our daughters walked down the street, smeared in artlessly applied make-up. And then we thought of how our other parent friends would react when, prompted by our girls, their daughters started asking for their own make-up kits.

But then, thinking about how others would react, we had an 'Aha' moment.

If we're being totally honest, our concerns about make-up weren't actually about our daughters. We were more worried about us. Our unease was really about how friends and strangers might respond to our decision to allow our daughters to play with make-up. We were afraid of having our own little real-life Kardashian take-down situation, and we were trying to control our daughters' bodies and appearance for our own benefit.

Body autonomy

Understanding the true motivation behind our reluctance to let our daughters buy make-up kits also brought with it the uncomfortable realisation that this decision was going against everything we try to teach our daughters about body autonomy.

Body autonomy is the idea that all of us, children included, own our bodies and have the right to make decisions about them. This applies particularly to girls – and the women they grow into.

Often girls and women are taught in thousands of different ways that their bodies exist for the pleasure of others, that they need to change their bodies or their appearance to fit in with whatever other people think is acceptable.

Girls are criticised for being too big or too small, for looking like Barbie, or for not making an effort. These are judgements that other people feel entitled to make about girls. As we mentioned in the previous chapter about body confidence, it is likely that your daughter has received more comments about her appearance than everything else combined. Unless parents deliberately counteract this pervasive message, girls will grow up believing that their bodies exist for other people, not themselves.

The guiding principle of body ownership

It sounds obvious and uncontroversial that a girl should own her body. Who doesn't want their daughter to own her own body? But granting girls ownership of their bodies is not something that we're good at doing in practice. We often have to fight against decades of our own programming and many of the expectations people still have about the role of children and our role as parents. It's one thing to *tell* your daughters that their bodies are their own and that they have the right to make decisions about them. Our actions often teach girls the opposite, that they are not at all autonomous when it comes to their bodies.

We don't just give girls mixed messages about make-up. We do it with clothes and jewellery and, as we'll see in a moment, even how they respond to other people's requests for affection.

Take ear piercing, for example. When Violet asked to get her ears pierced, the thoughts that automatically ran through our heads were, 'She's too young,' and 'She's growing up too quickly,' and then 'Is she going to set off an ear piecing trend in her peer group that will annoy the other parents?' Again, it wasn't so much about what it meant for Violet. Our opposition was based on what we thought was appropriate – and how we thought other people would react to our decision.

The same goes for clothes. A few years ago Violet decided to wear her favourite skirt to visit her grandparents. It was the most stained, torn and tattered skirt you could imagine. The elastic was frayed and it was a matted mess. But Violet loved it. Similarly, Ivy regularly opts to wear a bedazzled long black number with a pink frilly fishtail at the bottom. It wouldn't be out of place on a *Toddlers & Tiaras* runway. But if that's what she wants to wear, that's what she wears.

Do we sometimes wish our girls would make different clothing choices? Absolutely.

Would we override our girls' fashion choices? No way.

Some friends have commented that parents have a responsibility to intervene in order to teach their children what's appropriate to wear in different situations. Dressing 'nicely' is a sign of respect, particularly when children are in the presence of grandparents or attending formal gatherings.

While they may have a point, we think there is a bigger issue at stake. The larger lesson is that children, especially girls, should be allowed to be in charge of their appearance. Every time we tell girls that their clothing choice is wrong, we are diluting the importance of their decisions. We are telling them that our opinion about how they look is more valid than their own.

Guiding principle of body ownership

So where do you draw the line? Which of your daughter's choices about her appearance are acceptable and which are not? How do you decide when your daughter should make up her own mind about how she looks or when you should overrule her?

The guiding principle we use is: if it's not harmful and it's not permanent, then our daughter gets to decide and we will support her decision.

That's it. It's a simple rule but it can bring a lot of clarity to tricky situations.

The stipulation about harm is pretty straightforward. We don't want our girls to get hurt, so if they want to do something that we consider too dangerous then the answer is no.

By insisting that it isn't permanent, we are trying to save our girls from a decision that can't easily be undone, one that they may regret when they're older.

If our girls want to do something to or with their body that is not dangerous and not permanent, we support them, even if it's not our preference. That has included everything from decorating their faces with temporary tattoos to dyeing their hair. A permanent tattoo, of course, is out. For now.

Thinking back to ear piercing, ask yourself, 'Is ear piercing harmful, or is it permanent?' The answer is no, and no. Earrings can be taped or taken out for sports, making them harmless. And if our girls should decide later in life that they no longer want pierced ears, they can stop wearing earrings. All that will remain is a tiny little mark on their earlobes.

We used Violet's request for earrings to reinforce the message about body autonomy. 'It's your body so it's your choice.'

Of course, the very next day Violet went to school and told all her friends that she was getting her ears pierced. And that raised a few eyebrows with other parents. But if we had told Violet that she could not get her ears pierced, we would have been teaching her that she was not in charge of her body, that it was more important that her body pleased us rather than herself.

We sometimes counsel our girls when their wardrobe choices are going to restrict their ability to play. We don't know if you've ever seen a four-year-old try to climb an A-frame wearing a pancake tutu, the kind made of stiff tulle that sticks straight out, but it doesn't look easy. And fitting into a swing when you're wearing a mermaid's tail can be done but it's not particularly comfortable. But if our girls insist on wearing an outfit that does encumber them, they will inevitably make that discovery themselves. That in itself is a valuable lesson in body autonomy: if they want to wear big flouncy dresses, then they are going to limit their fun. And on many occasions, having learned the lesson firsthand, we've noticed that our girls often – not always, but often – make more practical clothing choices on future occasions.

'Harm' is not just physical

There is one caveat to the body-ownership principle. The caveat is this: what is harmful may not always be physical. Harm can also be psychological or social. Here, context is everything.

To give an example, a friend's seven-year-old daughter wanted to wax her legs. This came to a head when a classmate told the girl she was hairy. Actually, that's the kind version. This little girl was told that she was so hairy she looked like a monkey.

The mother was obviously conflicted. While she thought seven was too young to start waxing, she also hated to see her daughter suffer and wanted to help her feel better about herself. It's also difficult to tell your daughter that she can't wax her body hair when you're doing it yourself.

The mother asked us what we would do in her situation. We said that if it were our daughter we would not let her wax her legs. Of course, the process of waxing would not harm her daughter (and it's not permanent either), but encouraging a girl to change her body in response to someone else's opinion – let alone the opinion of a potential bully – does nothing to build body autonomy. On the contrary, it's the complete opposite of body autonomy.

For this girl, waxing her legs would not help her feel better about herself in the long run. All it would do is reinforce the idea that her body is so wrong that even her mum thinks it needs to be fixed.

If the classmate had told the girl that her lips were too thin, would the mother be considering collagen injections? What about if her daughter had dark skin and a kid told her she was too brown? Would we be discussing bleaching? Or would we let our seven-year-old drink diet shakes if some kid told her she was fat?

If we didn't live in a world that objectifies women and continually tells them their appearance isn't good enough, this wouldn't be such a big issue. But women are bombarded with messages about how they should and shouldn't look every day. These prescriptions about what is and what is not acceptable not only change constantly, they almost always come from someone else. Surrendering decisions about appearance to external sources is another way women are not in control of their bodies.

It's a tough lesson for a seven-year-old to learn, but imagine what a gift it would be to help your daughter realise that her acceptability is not determined by what the mean girl at school says about her body. Or what the ad on TV, or the boy she likes, or the magazine says is wrong with her body.

This is what we say to our daughters in these kinds of situations:

1. There will always be people who will try to tell you there is something wrong with you. Sometimes these people are being mean and want to hurt you. Other times they are trying to sell you something to fix the 'problem' they have told you that you have. In other cases, people are just clueless and are mindlessly repeating dumb things that have been said to them. What all of these have in common is that none of them is a good reason to change yourself. Have a look at your card about dealing with criticism (described in the Power Perspective chapter) and remind yourself that if this girl does not have your best interests at heart and if you don't respect her opinion, then she has not earned the right to be listened to.

2. Don't give someone else the power to decide if you are good enough. That is your right, your superpower. Don't give it up.

3. Everyone's body is different. Some bodies are tall, some are short. Some are fat, some are thin. We all come in different

.iurs. And, yes, some have more hair than others. None of these differences has anything to do with what sort of person you are. There is no such thing as a right body and a wrong body; there is just your body, and your body keeps you alive and allows you to swing on the monkey bars, laugh with your friends, and give us cuddles. There is nothing about your body that needs to be fixed.

But aren't kids growing up too fast these days?

That's all fine and good, you might be thinking, but shouldn't we be protecting girls' innocence? And aren't girls in particular being sexualised at a younger and younger age? Every couple of months there's another scandal about a department store carrying clothes aimed at girls that are degrading and objectifying. We've seen t-shirts with slogans like 'Future WAG', 'I Swallow', 'My Brain is 80% Song Lyrics' and 'Cute but Psycho'.

To be clear, we're not suggesting that the sexualisation of girls doesn't happen. Nor are we suggesting that such concerns are misplaced. On the contrary, there are many examples of companies encouraging girls to flaunt their 'sexuality' before they've had a chance to develop a sexual identity. We have as much concern as the next parent about raising girls within a culture that provides them with only two options: hot or not.

But there's a difference between the mass-produced and mass-marketed identities that are foisted upon girls, and what girls decide to do with their bodies to please themselves. One is just corporations preying on kids while the other is kids playing. Of course, that difference will depend on the context. Like all of us, girls don't make choices in isolation; they pick up on and internalise the attitudes, tastes and behaviours that surround them. Individuals do not grow up in a vacuum. We reflect and are affected by the culture we grow up in. Girls are shaped by advertising, the media and social media – just as we are.

It becomes a problem when a girl does what she thinks other people want her to do rather than what she wants because it's fun, or because she's curious, or role-playing. To give an example, one of our girls' friends started wearing a crop-top bra to school. She was six at the time. 'It's utterly ridiculous,' you might say. 'Little girls are growing up too fast. This child is being turned into a sex object.'

But ask yourself: who's the one turning this little girl into a sex object?

There's nothing inherently sexy about some material strapped around a little girl's torso. A six-year-old does not wear a bra to be sexy. At the age of six she may not have even heard the word, let alone understood the meaning of it. The girl's parents weren't putting her in pageants or that particularly creepy form of modelling where prepubescent girls are coached to make bedroom eyes to sell adult products. She wanted to wear a crop top because that's what Mummy wears. When a girl initiates it because she wants to be like Mummy or to play grown-ups, it's innocent. It's no different from when our daughters want to dress in 'lady' clothes, clip-clop around in high-heeled shoes, or carry handbags. It's hardly surprising that this little girl wanted to wear the same underwear as her mother. By projecting our value judgements onto a child, we turn a piece of clothing into a moral panic.

When we prohibit a little girl from dressing this way, we are, yet again, sending the message that she has no right to control her body. We are telling her that what other people think she should do with her body is more important than what she wants to do with it. And we're implicitly telling her that it's okay to judge a woman's character by the clothes she wears. If we're really concerned about protecting our girls' innocence then we should be shielding them from these attitudes, not helping to instil them.

The same applies to make-up. The Kardashian backlash was based on the assumption that a girl's or woman's motivation for wearing make-up is to please men, rather than herself. The rules about 'acceptable' make-up on girls are messed up. Why is lip gloss okay but lipstick is not? Why can a girl paint her toenails without her mother being trolled, but not her mouth? A girl can wear a full face of expertly applied make-up for a dance concert and no one says anything. But if a little girl clumsily smears some lipstick on her eyebrows she's 'growing up too fast'.

The notion that pigment applied to a girl's lips will destroy her innocence, setting her on a path to ruin, is not only ridiculous, it's also uncomfortably close to people blaming girls and women when they are the victims of assault. It perpetuates the idea that make-up – especially red lipstick – is a sexual invitation to men, or that a girl or woman wearing make-up is 'asking for it'.

Watching our delighted girls play with their make-up kits taught us that the question about when girls are old enough to wear make-up is misguided. It's not the 'when' that matters but the 'why'. The same applies to crop-top bras.

Why do girls want to dress in crop-top bras? If girls dressing up in bras, or anything else for that matter, is fun for them, and – crucially – is initiated by them, rather than some external expectation, then it is not harmful. In fact, by prohibiting these kinds of activities, we run the risk of sexualising something that is innocent, and reframing a game into an exercise in shaming and disempowerment.

Why did our girls want to play with make-up? Not because they are sexualising themselves or self-objectifying. Not because they are disguising their 'flaws' or trying to please someone. For them, make-up is play, a fun form of creative self-expression. Even the red lipstick.

Little girls and kisses

So far, we've focused on girls controlling their own appearance. But body autonomy is about more than how a girl dresses or what she chooses to put on her face. Just as relevant – and arguably much more important – is whether she gets to make decisions about expressing affection and intimacy.

This is where, for many parents, body autonomy gets tougher. Much tougher. How tough? Let's look at the following example.

Kasey's story

A few years ago, a man serving me coffee in my regular cafe said to Violet, 'Give us a kiss.'

Inside, I was screaming, 'Don't ask my daughter to kiss you! It's creepy!'

I remember being presented with cheeks when I was a kid and feeling the discomfort of such forced intimacy. Despite my own bad experiences from childhood, I didn't intervene on Violet's behalf. I stood by silently and watched as my little girl hesitated, flinched and then obliged.

As far as I could tell, the man wasn't being predatory. I didn't want to offend him or cause a scene. I was being the people-pleasing Good Girl that I'm trying to teach my girls not to be. I prioritised social harmony and appeasing a relative stranger over the wishes of my daughter.

I was wrong.

By remaining silent and acquiescing to a stranger's request for Violet's affection, I effectively told my daughter, 'It's okay to say no – unless you make someone else feel awkward or embarrassed and then it's not okay to say no.'

That is a confusing message even for an adult. It must be utterly bewildering for a child. If there's one lesson we've learned about children, especially young children, it's that they don't do subtlety. Most of the time kids work in absolutes. Subtlety comes later.

When it comes to affection, girls need to know that if they don't want to kiss somebody – or be kissed by somebody – then they shouldn't have to. In order for our girls to feel confident in exerting ownership over their bodies and refusing someone's request for affection, they need to know that we as their parents will always back them up unequivocally, no matter how embarrassing this will be for us, or for the person asking for a kiss.

On this occasion in the cafe, and on all the occasions before, I should have stepped in and modelled to Violet that it's okay to say no, even when it's socially awkward.

The high five policy

We thought a lot about the implications of that kissing incident in the cafe and what it was teaching Violet about who really owns her body. (Not her.) From that moment on, we decided we would not only never ask our girls to kiss anyone they don't want to, but also actively help them develop socially acceptable strategies to politely navigate these situations. Now, when someone demands kisses from our girls we suggest they give the kiss-requester a high five or a hand-shake instead. Lucy Emmerson, the director of the Sex Education Forum in the UK, recommends that parents give children a selection of alternatives to choose from. 'Intervening may be awkward . . . but it is necessary if we are truly to teach children that their bodies are their own and that their instincts should be followed,' Emmerson says. 'Suggesting alternatives to the child such as a high five, a hug, blowing a kiss or a wave puts the child in control.'[1]

Australian sexuality educator Margie Buttriss says that without guidance it can be difficult for children to know how to respond to unwanted affection. 'We're talking about situations such as when Grandma wants to swoop in for the big sloppy kiss and if the child doesn't want that to happen what can they do,' she said. '[T]hey can respectfully say "No thanks, Grandma, let's have a hug instead."' In a situation where the child does not know the person demanding affection, Buttriss also recommends kids offer a high five or a fist bump.[2]

These options give children more choices about how they want to respond to friendly advances. Children are introduced to the world of civil graces, recognising and acknowledging others, while also putting boundaries in place. Girls should take for granted that they have the right to say no – even if it causes offence. Personal boundaries should be taught – early and consistently.

Each request for affection is an opportunity to reinforce the message – both in practice as well as in theory – that the only person who decides who your daughter kisses/hugs is her.

Taking things too far?

No doubt some would say our high five policy is taking things too far. We've been called 'the kissing police' and accused of teaching our girls to be rude. Our family decision not to force our girls to kiss people made international headlines. One woman told us that by our standard, she wouldn't be able to kiss her grandchild and that would break her heart.

To be clear, we're not suggesting that grandparents are sexual predators. Nor are we saying that children shouldn't be affectionate with grandparents or other relatives and family friends. Our girls love to hug and snuggle with their grandparents and other important adults in their lives. We encourage this.

Some families and cultures are more physically affectionate than others. We are not suggesting there is anything wrong with this type of affection. In fact, in many cases it's lovely, warm and affirming. But this is not an issue of affection – it's an issue of *choice* and who gets to make that choice. If a girl wants to kiss and cuddle her grandmother then that's wonderful. If she doesn't want to then we believe that she shouldn't be forced to. Hopefully Granny will understand that her granddaughter's right to own her body is more important than Grandma's (or anyone else's) desire for physical affection.

While these demands may be innocent and harmless with grandparents, that's not always going to be the case. Cast your mind a few years into the future when your daughter will face other requests and demands for affection that will not be as innocent and well intentioned as Granny's. What about when she gets her first job as a waitress and a sleazy customer slides his hand up her skirt? Should she just put up with it because she doesn't want to be rude or cause offence? What about when your daughter is with a boyfriend who's pressuring her for sex? What about when the cool boy at school demands she send him a nude selfie? The research tells us that the vast majority of girls are grossly unprepared for these situations. A study published in the journal *Sexuality Research and Social Policy* entitled '"What Should I Do?": Young women's reported dilemmas with nude photographs' found that of the nearly 500 girls aged 12–18 years surveyed who'd sent explicit photos of themselves, only 8 per cent of them had actually wanted to send them. The other 92 per cent of girls did it because of a desire to please, to acquiesce, or to avoid conflict with a boy.[3]

Some people may object that it's a pretty big leap from an affectionate kiss for Grandma to being pressured by a boyfriend to send nudes. But, again, this isn't about affection. It's about body autonomy. It's about a girl's capacity to control her own body. Even when it causes offence.

The ritual of demanding instant affection from children is one of those tiny, everyday lessons in which we teach children – especially girls – that they should tailor their emotional responses to please others. A girl quickly learns that it's more important she doesn't upset Grandpa (or Grandma, or her uncle or aunt) than it is for her to feel comfortable. A girl must do something with her body she doesn't want to do to please someone else. The lesson: the girl does not own her body.

Unless we take corrective action, she may carry this lesson with her throughout her life.

Body ownership takes practice

Do we think that kids will just know how to drive a car on their sixteenth birthday? Of course not. We teach them. We make sure that they learn with experienced drivers and trained instructors and that they have opportunities to practise these new skills in safe situations. We encourage them to experience driving in city traffic, and on freeways and open roads. We teach parking and turning, lane changes and changing gears. We make sure that kids have hours of driving practice under their belt before heading out on the roads by themselves.

When it comes to bodily ownership, though, we act as though it's something that kids suddenly 'get' on their sixteenth or eighteenth or whatever birthday. What's worse, from day one, families may have been teaching girls the opposite: that they must use their bodies to please other people. How do we expect girls to magically unlearn this lesson when the stakes are high?

Often without realising it, parents can link their approval and affection for their daughter with her behaviour of pleasing other people, be it through her appearance or compliance with unwanted kisses. When girls do exercise ownership over their own bodies, they may sense disappointment from their families for 'causing a scene' or making other people feel awkward. In short, we tend to connect social approval, and even affection, with our daughters complying with everyone else's wishes, regardless of what they themselves want.

If a girl has never been able to practise body ownership in the safe confines of family relationships and friendships – if she has always been told that she has to please others and not make waves – then she's unlikely to feel she can enforce her boundaries when it comes to other relationships – especially romantic and sexual ones.

If you listen to girls who say they felt pressure to provide sex or intimacy to boys, you often hear that they didn't feel as if they had a choice. One fourteen-year-old participant in the '"What Should I Do?": Young women's reported dilemmas with nude photographs' study mentioned above said, 'My bf pressured me for hours to send him pictures of me naked. Now he threatens to send them out if I don't send him more really nasty pics. The stuff I have to do is unbelievable.'[4]

Note that this girl says, 'the stuff I *have* to do'. She feels she has no choice but to send pictures of herself naked, because her boyfriend will punish her if she doesn't. That is the definition of an abusive relationship. One reason that such abuse starts and then escalates is that many girls do not feel they have body autonomy. If she had a greater sense of ownership of her own body, she may not have sent the photos in the first place and given him an opportunity to blackmail her. Of course, a big part of the problem here is her boyfriend's expectation that his girlfriend exists to please him. But at the same time, she feels as if she has no other option but to cave in to the pressure. Another alarming component to this situation is that the girl didn't turn to her family for help. It's possible that if body autonomy has never been modelled in this girl's family, she would assume that her parents wouldn't support her.

Many girls are conditioned to feel as though their body is not their own. It's what we teach girls from their earliest days. And we teach them this in the most innocent and unremarkable settings – like family gatherings. We effectively tell girls that it's utterly normal for them to provide affection to others, in spite of what their actual wishes may be.

What is surprising is that, having told girls all their lives that their role is to make others feel okay, we then blame them for making poor choices when they hit teenagehood and their hormones are raging. Given that we've taught them to please others, why would we expect them to suddenly do otherwise?

One in three think your daughter shouldn't own her body

In 2017 Girl Scouts of America advised parents not to force their daughter to give affection.[5] 'Have you ever insisted, "Uncle just got here – go give him a big hug!" or "Auntie gave you that nice toy, go give her a kiss," when you were worried your child might not offer affection on her own?' the organisation published on their website in the lead-up to the holiday season.

> If yes, you might want to reconsider the urge to do that in the future. Think of it this way, telling your child that she owes someone a hug either just because she hasn't seen this person in a while or because they gave her a gift can set the stage for her questioning whether she 'owes' another person any type of physical affection when they've bought her dinner or done something else seemingly nice for her later in life.

Just as we have experienced ourselves, the Girl Scouts received considerable backlash after they issued this advice. The *Today* show in the US ran a poll on whether people agreed with the Girl Scouts' advice and one third of respondents said 'no'.[6]

This suggests that when it comes to girls, body autonomy remains a controversial issue. If we want to teach our girls that they do in fact own their bodies, we need to take clear and deliberate steps to instil this belief.

Her body ownership is more important than your comfort

Be prepared to feel awkward and embarrassed. The first time someone demands a kiss from your daughter, who squirms with discomfort, and you intervene with, 'How about a high five?', there may well be consequences. Breaking a script that has been running in your family for generations is not for the faint-hearted.

But if we want to raise girls who like themselves then we have to risk upsetting the family dynamic. It is evidently not enough to just *tell* our girls that they own their bodies and that they don't have to do what other people wish. We want our girls to know, through years of experience, that they can make an unpopular decision about their bodies and they will still be loved and accepted by us. If a girl is to truly have body ownership then she must know that she is free to make her choice, even when some of the important people in her life don't like her decision.

One way to overcome the potential awkwardness with family and friends is to speak openly with them about your new high five policy and explain the reasons behind it. Tell them that if your daughter *chooses* to offer physical affection that's great, but if she doesn't then accepting and encouraging her body autonomy is important to you and your daughter's wellbeing – now and in the future. Some people may push back. Given that you're up against decades, even centuries, of cultural conditioning about how girls and women are expected to behave and respond, it would be surprising if it didn't cause a few ripples with some people in your life. That's okay. People don't have to agree with your choices about how you raise your daughter. You don't need their approval – but you do need them to respect your decisions – and those of your daughter.

It's not just friends and family either. We as parents also need to respect and honour our daughters' decisions when *we* don't agree with them. In fact, it's more important than ever that parents follow through with their commitment to their daughter's body autonomy when she makes choices that are different from our own. When our girls want to do something with their bodies that we don't agree with – for example, when Violet refused to cut her hair even though it was so long it was a tangled, knotted nightmare, or when Ivy wanted to wear her snorkel, mask and nightie to a cafe – we tell them, 'It wouldn't be my choice, but it's not my choice. It's your body so it's your choice.' We come back to the guiding principle of body autonomy: if it's not dangerous and it's not permanent, then our girls get to decide.

It's not always easy to bite our tongues at some of our girls' choices. But the greater lesson of body ownership is far more important than any temporary, non-harmful decision our girls may make about their bodies.

Name all body parts

The Chinese philosopher Confucius was once asked what the first priority of a new ruler should be. He replied, 'to rectify names'. In today's terms, we would say, 'to call things by their proper names'.

What applies to rulers applies equally to us when it comes to being masters of our own bodies. Many of us were raised in families where our body parts, particularly genitals, didn't even have a name. It was 'down there' or 'private parts' or, at best, 'front bottom' and 'back bottom'. This makes about as much sense as calling arms 'swingy parts' or legs 'walky bits'.

No matter how relaxed you think you are with the subject of genitalia, if you can't even bring yourself to use the correct terms, kids will see straight through it. It follows that if we want our daughter to feel as comfortable possessing a vulva and vagina as she does about her arms and legs, then a necessary first step is to give them the correct names.

Correctly naming your daughter's genitalia is not just about pride or being anatomically correct. It's also for your daughter's protection and safety. If a child is being abused by an adult or another child, they need to be able to talk about what's happening to them in terms that are easily and clearly understood by adults. If your daughter's genitalia is something that is never spoken about, she will not have the language or the confidence to tell you if something 'bad is happening to it'. Using euphemisms for genitals, especially words that are used only within the confines of your family, also increases the likelihood that a child will be misunderstood if she seeks help from people outside of the family, such as teachers or doctors.[7]

Lyba Spring, a sex educator from Canada, has seen how incorrect terminology has led to the continuation of abuse. 'The only word [a girl] knew for vulva was "cookie". When she tried to tell a teacher about how someone wanted her cookie, the teacher told her she had to share. It's obvious that the consequence of that was that the abuse continued. She didn't have the tools she needed to disclose.'

Knowing the correct terminology for body parts may even prevent the abuse from happening in the first place. Research shows that some sexual offenders avoid children who know the correct names for their genitals because it suggests these children are more educated and aware of body safety.[8]

Make sure she knows what real genitals look like

On our bookshelves, nestled between books about fairies and zoo animals, are books about the human body and puberty. Within these pages are illustrations of genitalia and reproductive organs. This has raised some eyebrows among friends. What if other children see them? Wouldn't it be traumatic for a child to see such graphic imagery? Just to clarify, we're not talking about pornography here. We are talking about anatomically correct illustrations of body parts. The idea that a young girl would be traumatised by seeing a picture of a vulva and a vagina harks back to the days of the women's liberation movement of the 1960s, when it was considered radical for women to get a mirror and inspect their genitals. It seems bizarre now that a woman could reach adulthood without having once taken a look at a part of her own body.

But in many respects not much has changed in the last fifty years. Vaginas are still a source of secrecy, shame and misinformation. In a world of porn and photoshopped images of female genitalia, girls are growing up believing that Barbie is anatomically correct and a natural vulva is gross. When these girls don't measure up to the

Mattel ideal, they feel like freaks and increasingly go to extreme lengths to deal with what they see as their 'disfigurement', such as labiaplasty, the trimming of the inner and outer labia.

A worldwide study of general practitioners revealed that the number of girls under the age of eighteen requesting cosmetic surgery on their labias is on the rise. In Australia, requests have tripled since 2003. In many cases, these girls' vulvas had not fully developed and there was nothing actually wrong with their genitals.[9]

It's also important that girls understand they have three holes: a urethra for wee, a vagina for babies (the mechanics of baby-making can come later) and an anus for poo.

Speaking openly to their daughters about female genitals can be really hard for parents of our generation who were raised with secrecy and shame, but unless we find a way to overcome our own hang-ups we will very likely pass them on to our girls. Getting comfortable in their own skin is an important step towards empowerment.

Masturbation

We hate to break it to you, but children masturbate. Yep, even your daughter.

It may sound entirely obvious, but many parents seem to be in denial about this – or think that they can simply make it go away. For example, we once overheard a mother explaining to a group of mothers at the park that she 'caught' her preschooler 'touching herself'.

'So I told her,' the mother continued, 'that her bottom is dirty and she should never ever touch it.'

A quick search online also reveals that this woman isn't the only one who thinks it's a good idea to tell girls that parts of their bodies are 'dirty'.

'My daughter is five and has recently began exploring herself [sic],' writes a concerned mother in a mothers' Facebook group. 'I've caught her doing the same thing to her clitoris in the bath and I've also caught her putting her blankey between her legs and rocking . . . I told her that we must remember that our bodies are special and what she is doing isn't in the best interest of her body because she could hurt herself.' Another mother adds, 'I just say, "Your bottom isn't a toy. It's special and you need to stop playing with it."' This is followed up by another mother with, 'I don't allow masturbation in my home.'

While it's deluded to believe that you can simply outlaw masturbation by decree, this view is not surprising given the sexual embarrassment and discomfort that is handed down through the generations in families. Historically, women have been taught to regard their genitals with shame and embarrassment. As Nancy Friday wrote in *My Mother/My Self*, 'Sexual self-discovery is the only self-discovery that is not celebrated in infancy and childhood. The day the child learns to eat with a spoon, everyone says, "Isn't it wonderful? Someone get the Polaroid!" But the day she discovers her vagina, nobody says, "It's six months earlier than it should have been, isn't she a precious darling!"'[10]

Friday's book first appeared in 1977 but her message is as important and as relevant now as it was the day it was published. It's normal and healthy for children to explore their bodies. It feels good to touch your clitoris, so of course girls are going to want to do it. Trying to outlaw masturbation is not only ineffectual, but also reinforces the notion that girls are not in charge of their bodies and that they aren't entitled to pleasure for pleasure's sake. It perpetuates the stereotype of women being passive: they are not allowed to meet their own needs, and must therefore rely on somebody else (a man) to take care of them.

There's a time and a place

However, children also need to learn that it's not socially acceptable for kids (or anyone for that matter) to masturbate in public.

Our challenge as parents is to teach our girls about the rules of self-exploration without burdening them with shame and a sense of disempowerment over their bodies. We approach this from the perspective of 'there's a time and a place for everything'. We all know how to teach our kids that there are some times and places they can be loud and boisterous and other times and places where they must be quiet, without instilling shame and embarrassment. These rules may take patience and a lot of reinforcement to teach, but they are pretty straightforward and uncomplicated. Apply the same approach to masturbation. The time and place for masturbation is when a person is on their own, in private. It's just another 'time and place' rule for kids to file away with all the other 'time and place' rules.

If you're having trouble finding the words – which is understandable since they were probably never said to you as a child – here is a suggestion of what to say. When you see your daughter touching her clitoris, tell her what it is. For example: 'That's your clitoris. It feels good when you touch it. Grown-up women touch their clitorises too. The rule about your clitoris is that you only play with it when you are alone, like in your bedroom.'

This lets your daughter know that masturbation is normal, that women do it, while ensuring that she understands that there's an appropriate time and place. The next time you see your daughter touching her clitoris in public, just gently remind her of the rule. For example: 'Remember the rule about your clitoris? You only play with it when you are on your own, like when you're in your bedroom by yourself.'

Get over your squeamishness for your daughter's sake

Having children and having to deal with these issues may make some parents realise that they are not nearly as sexually liberated as they might have thought. Despite our own personal discomfort, our aim should be to raise our daughters without shame, fear or embarrassment around their genitals. If we accept that a girl who likes herself believes she owns her body, it follows that she owns her sex organs too. Given the culture and history of ignorance, shame and embarrassment about women's sexuality and genitals, the only way she will unlearn this lesson is if we break the cycle of sexual silence and shame.

Action for dads

Teach your daughter about body autonomy through play.

One of the most important lessons you can impart to your daughter is that 'no' always means 'no'. This sounds simple and obvious. Yet it is something that we need to teach and continually reinforce. One way to do so is through play, such as common tickling and rough-and-tumble games that fathers play with their daughters. If you are tickling your daughter and she is squealing, 'No, no, stop it, Daddy,' stop immediately.

She may, at that point, ask why you stopped. If she does, you can tell her that she told you to stop. For example, you might say to your daughter, 'I stopped tickling you because you said no. If you ask someone to stop it, they have to stop it straight away.' By doing so, you're showing her that she has a right to expect this from other people in her life. You're telling her that her wishes are important, that she shouldn't be worried or fearful about expressing them.

If you don't stop after she has asked you to, you may be unintentionally teaching her that she has no right to expect her wishes to be heard or complied with. You might also be training her to believe that it is acceptable for someone who is bigger than her to physically overpower her – even when she asks them not to.

Many dads are horrified by the suggestion that play could be construed in this way. But play is where children learn. Children, especially young children, are often not capable of understanding nuance. They can't necessarily see the distinction between a game with Daddy where it's okay for 'no' to mean 'keep going', and other contexts where it's not okay. Children think in absolutes and if you want your daughter to have the courage and confidence to say 'no' and mean it to other men and boys, then you are the best person to teach this to her.

Recap

- Your daughter is going to be confronted with many situations in her life where someone will try to control or use her body. It might be the friend who tells her she needs to go on a diet. It could be the social media influencer or the beauty, weight-loss and fashion industries who will manipulate her for profit. It could be the boyfriend who pressures her for nude selfies or demands oral sex. It could be the boss who likes to give her a 'massage' at her desk. We cannot protect our daughter from all of the toxic experiences she's likely to encounter, but we can prepare her to deal with them in the best way she can by teaching her that she – and only she – has the right to decide what happens to her body, and to expect others to respect her wishes where her body is concerned.
- Words are not enough. We need to model body autonomy, teach it and seek out opportunities for our daughter to practise enforcing the ownership of her body. This needs to happen even – and especially – when it makes us parents uncomfortable. This includes supporting her right not to give affection to adults, and allowing her to make her own decisions about what she wears, how she cuts her hair and how she looks. Remember, the guiding principle is: if it's not harmful and it's not permanent then your daughter gets to decide. Our job as parents is to support her decision and her right to make it.
- A girl cannot have full ownership of her body if she is ashamed of it or embarrassed by it. Give genitals their correct names and

refer to these body parts with the same ease you would have discussing any other body part, such as arms or legs.

- Reinforce the rule that 'no' always means 'no' by complying with her wishes and not allowing any tickling or chasing games where girls say 'no' and the (usually) bigger and stronger boys and men override her request and ignore her wishes. Play is where children learn, and this is where important lessons about body autonomy begin.

4

A girl who likes
herself is calm

Our generation of parents seems to be more invested in our children's performance and development than any other in history. Fifty years ago, if your kid was alive and fed at the end of the day then you could pat yourself on the back for a job well done. But we now pour an extraordinary amount of our time, money and energy into helping our kids achieve milestones early, thrash their friends on the sporting field, get higher marks on their tests, get their black belts sooner, and play instruments more proficiently. For many, childhood has become an endless self-improvement boot camp.

When it comes to the pursuit of extracurricular activities and 'learning opportunities', parental anxieties run deep. It's not unusual for girls to do lessons such as ballet, martial arts, gymnastics, academic tutoring, athletics, tennis, piano, basketball, drama or violin, with something on every afternoon after school or preschool. In order to maintain this lifestyle, families are scheduled like an air traffic control tower. Every minute is accounted for, not a moment is wasted, in a delicate balance of interdependencies. If you think everything seems busier now than it was in the past, you're right. In 2013, Swedish furniture manufacturer IKEA commissioned a report that found nearly half (47 per cent) of Australian children do three or more after-school activities each week. When the 1400 kids and parents who responded to the 'Time to Live Report' were asked to recall the previous month, 43 per cent said they hadn't done anything spontaneous.[1]

We've seen it in our friendship group. Some primary-school girls do so many extracurricular activities they are not home before 7.30 pm on weeknights. Some eat their dinner in the car as they are taxied from one activity to the next. Others eat so late that their parents tell us they are falling asleep at the table as food is shovelled into their mouths. After a full day of childcare some of Ivy's little friends were picked up by their conscientious – and exhausted – parents and taken to gym classes and music lessons. And then these girls do more classes or formal sport on the weekend. Parents feel like they alternate between being Uber drivers and sergeant majors for their kids as they rush and nag them in order to get to each appointment on time. Then they brace themselves for the bedtime routine, when everyone is frazzled and at their worst. The whole family is cranky and strung out when they fall into bed each night. And then they get up in the morning and do it all over again.

While this constant stress and pressure might be normal and even appropriate in air traffic control towers, it's a shortcut to sucking the joy and fun out of family life. Very often it can turn our daughters (and us too!) into exhausted, anxious balls of stress.

Why, then, do we do it? Many parents fervently believe that this level of intense activity is maximising their daughter's potential and optimising her opportunities in life. They sacrifice, often without intending to, their daughter's sleep, playtime and spontaneity in pursuit of these aims. This is not to mention the loss of their own sanity and hard-earned income. Until recently we over-scheduled our girls, too. The pressure to 'enhance' our children is so intense and pervasive that, like so many other parents, we found it difficult to resist. We thought this was what good parenting looked like. But we believe we got it wrong.

In this chapter we will show you that cramming as many skills and experiences into your daughter as possible, like a goose at a foie gras farm, does not create the conditions required to raise a girl who likes herself. We think it's time for parents to find the courage to push back against the culture of intense parenting. In essence, we need to back off and slow down because a girl who likes herself is not overtired, overstressed, overextended or overscheduled. A girl who likes herself is calm.

When we talk about girls being calm, we are not referring to children who are super Zen, quiet, obedient or obliging. Our girls are just as likely to use their 'outside voices' in a quiet waiting room or do an ill-timed cartwheel down a busy supermarket aisle as much as any other girl. By calm, we mean creating a life for girls where they have time and space to get off the self-improvement treadmill to enjoy more unstructured time, where they can be children, rather than learning machines.

Why does modern parenting resemble foie gras farming?

It's not surprising that parents fall into the trap of over-scheduling their kids. Even before a child is born, expectant parents are flooded with brochures displaying savvy marketing from companies cashing in on parental anxieties. We have apps to track developmental milestones, telling us what our kids should be doing by what age. Any tardiness on the child's part in meeting – or surpassing – the milestone is a cause for minor panic. And it just doesn't let up. Entrepreneurial 'experts' pry open parents' wallets with talk of 'brain development' and 'self-esteem' and giving your child a 'head start'. What parent wouldn't want all this for their daughter?

We fell for it as hard as anyone. When Violet was six months old we booked her into swimming lessons. We didn't have hopes of her competing at the Olympics or anything like that. We just figured that as we live in a country that is an island, being able to swim is a must. We were also suckers for the marketing spiel about how baby swimming lessons would enhance cognitive function, muscle development and parent–child bonding.

Violet hated her first lesson and screamed all the way through it. We chalked that up to it all being new. The second lesson was no different. Again, we told ourselves she was just adjusting. But it didn't get any better for the rest of the term. She made it clear – as only a six-month-old can – that she hated the whole experience. She wasn't the only one. We hated it too. All she learned from those first lessons was to scream whenever she saw water. But we stupidly persisted with it because we thought that's just what good parents did. Eventually we realised that, while it's important that kids learn how to swim, Violet didn't need to acquire this particular skill in the first six months of her life. We decided we did not need a structured, expert-led swimming lesson in order to bond with her or to keep her physical and cognitive development on track.

The not-so-subtle message put out by those selling these services is that it's not enough to simply raise a daughter any-more. Good parents have to enhance her. Parents have been sold the lie that more extracurricular activities are always better, no matter how much they may disrupt a family's daily routine or eat into downtime. We're taught that kids' brains are little sponges primed to soak up as much information as we can throw their way. Cramming as much knowledge, skills and experience into our children as early as possible is now considered one of the key measures of good parenting.

The pressure to enhance our girls has become even stronger with the rise of social media and Insta-perfect children. There's an infinite scroll of overachieving children who appear to split their time between winning merit certificates, dazzling at dance concerts, and scoring goals. There are so many above-average children featured on Facebook that it appears Mark Zuckerberg has invented a platform that has altered the laws of mathematics. Meanwhile, the only skill *your* child seems intent on perfecting is making fart noises under her armpit. Any time you get a camera out she puts a finger up her nose or pokes her tongue out. The app to make those pics social-media friendly hasn't yet been invented.

This fear that your daughter is underperforming compared with her apparently perfect peers can exacerbate the legitimate anxieties parents have about their daughters' future financial security, as a result of insecure workplaces, the rising cost of education and the affordability of home ownership. In fact, 'downtime' has come to be equated with 'wasted time'. If children aren't engaged in some structured activity to perfect their artistic ability, improve their language or numeracy skills, or develop their physical dexterity, it's almost as if their childhood is being negligently squandered and their future health, happiness and prosperity put at risk. It's therefore not surprising that extracurricular activities have become an arms race as parents fear that their daughter will miss out if they don't join in.

But ask yourself: if you take a stand and refuse to participate in this arms race, what is your daughter really missing out on?

Will your daughter really miss out?

A couple of years ago we received an email from a gymnastics club about tryouts for their elite squad. Depending on their skill level, the girls who were selected for the squad would be required to train 7.5–20 hours per week and potentially compete in regional competitions. The girls who didn't get into the squad were welcome to do non-competitive gymnastics classes for just 1–2 hours per week. This email was a sobering moment for us in the frenzy that extracurricular activities had become.

Violet would have loved to try out for squad but we decided against it, and instead signed her up for the one-hour class. Of course, she may not have even got into the squad, but if she had been selected it would have overstretched both her and us. Spending 20 hours a week on an extracurricular activity is a huge commitment, on top of school and all the other things she needs to do. Having a superior backflip is hard to justify if she is a tired wreck for everything else. So by not trying out for squad, by not training for up to 20 hours a week, what exactly did our daughter miss out on?

We're not suggesting that extracurricular activities or elite sports are bad. Perhaps gymnastics is your daughter's and your family's passion and you all love nothing more than spending your free time doing gymnastics. If it suits your daughter and your family then go for it. But if it becomes too consuming, to the point that it puts your daughter and your family under stress, then you have to ponder whether it is worthwhile. If these activities block out other parts of your daughter's childhood, then it may not be worth it. Ask yourself this question about any extracurricular activity your daughter might do: in the greater scheme of her life, what is she really missing out on if she doesn't do it?

'But she loves it'

Parents have told us that they'd happily reduce their daughter's activities but she loves the activity so much she'd be disappointed if she had to stop. This may be true. But the same argument can be made for ice cream. Or TV and iPads. Just because a child loves something doesn't mean it's necessarily good for them. As the saying goes, the dose makes the poison. Have too much of anything, even good stuff, and it becomes toxic. As parents it's our job to make these decisions and put boundaries in place, even if it does result in tears and disappointment.

It's about getting the balance right. If you and your daughter are both chronically tired and rushed, and she feels constant pressure to be 'on' and perform, then something's out of whack. While our girls and their peers may be the most accomplished generation in history, glance back to our Report Card on page xvi and you will see that they are also arguably the most unhappy, insecure and anxious. Rushing our children from one activity to the next, turning every moment into an adult-approved and -led 'learning opportunity' is not contributing to raising girls who like themselves.

Georgina Manning, director of Wellbeing for Kids, says that she has seen a dramatic increase in anxiety and emotional distress in children due to over-scheduling. Manning, who is a registered counsellor and psychotherapist, says:

> Rushing children around and filling every spare moment of their lives with 'interesting' activities doesn't teach children how to manage stress. It just creates stressed-out kids. This is not at all to blame parents, it's just a fact we can't ignore. It doesn't mean our home needs to always be peaceful as this is not realistic, but overall if there is a sense of calm then this creates space for creativity, play, conversation and a place to just rest, which in turn helps children to rest their brain. If children are not rested with time for play and fun then they don't have a chance to wind down, reflect, play and de-stress the brain.

You might also be wasting your money and your – and your daughter's – time. When kids are tired they cannot learn properly, so you may be exposing your daughter to all these new opportunities but they're not being absorbed because she is too exhausted.

But what about commitment?

Parents have told us that if they were to cancel their daughter's extracurricular activities it would teach her a very poor lesson about commitment. They don't want to raise a quitter. This is especially the case when it comes to team sports, where other children are relying on their daughter.

We are not advocating that your daughter should be encouraged to just not show up whenever she can't be bothered going. Instead, make sure that when she opts to do an extracurricular activity, she understands that she is committing – and you are most likely paying – for the entire term. Once that term is over, then you as a family can reassess your daughter's schedule and make any necessary changes. This gives her some choice and control about how she spends her time, while also teaching her about keeping her commitments.

The importance of play

One of the first casualties in the life of an over-scheduled child is play. We often don't appreciate just how important it is. We refer to activities and pursuits that we regard as easy as 'child's play', as if they are so trivial as to be hardly worth bothering with. People tend to treat play as a frivolous luxury that kids can do if there is a spare moment after they've finished doing all their important learning activities.

If children are allowed to play at all, we feel more comfortable if it is a structured, measured, expert-endorsed, adult-led activity. But this isn't really play at all – it's structured learning dressed up to look like play. True play is about free and spontaneous expression. It's about allowing children to create and become absorbed in exploring their own little worlds for no other reason than the pleasure of doing so. That last bit is important. When children play, in the true sense of the word, their play doesn't have any goal or motive other than itself. When children are really playing they are not trying to achieve anything in particular. The goal of play – to the extent that it can be said to have a goal at all – is simply the delight in doing it. This is the difference, for example, between kicking a ball around the backyard with friends and going to a soccer coaching clinic where the objective is to improve match performance.

In true play, kids should get lost in the task. Psychologists call this flow. 'Flow is when they totally lose track of time and have full engagement in enjoyable activities that don't necessarily have an outcome or are achievement-based, such as winning a game,' says Georgina Manning. Examples of flow activities might include constructing Lego, drawing, creating or building something where you switch off the outside world, playing with friends, imagination games, reading, sport that doesn't have a focus on winning, and, crucially, activities instigated by the child, rather than those that are adult-directed. 'Ideally, children should experience "flow" most days,' Manning suggests.

As you'll see in the next section, this true form of play is critical if you want to raise a girl who likes herself. Giving your daughter the gift of play is going to be far more valuable to her physical and emotional wellbeing and development than perfecting her somersault or pirouette.

Play is the 'work' of childhood

Talking up the benefits of play seems like a scandalous waste of time in a world that is obsessed with grades, competition and outward markers of achievement. It's particularly controversial given that we're constantly being told that the current generation of kids is slipping in international rankings for science, maths and reading. Shouldn't we be doing everything we can to link play to some other 'higher' purpose, like learning a second language or sneakily adding in some maths games to improve their numeracy?

But trying to redesign play so that it accomplishes some adult-approved purpose defeats the point of play in the first place. The good news is that you don't need to make play a learning activity because it already is one. Jordan Shapiro is an assistant professor at Temple University and has a background in psychology. He writes that play 'is the work of childhood'.[2] It is through play that children's brains evolve; play is how they develop their creativity, acquire the ability to process and retain information, regulate their emotions, and manage their behaviour.[3] It's also how they learn to get along with others – something that's crucial for later in life when they have to get along in workplaces and public spaces. Australian parenting author and educator Maggie Dent says that play has emotional, social, cognitive and spiritual benefits. 'We know that play allows children to take risks, make mistakes, learn to wait, solve problems, and – very importantly – to learn to win and lose graciously,' Dent writes in *Real Kids in an Unreal World*.[4]

Not only does play teach your daughter critical academic and life skills, it also prepares her brain for formal learning. Think of it like repairing an overloaded computer hard drive or, to put it non-technically, when your phone or computer gets overwhelmed and starts playing up. Resetting your frozen or malfunctioning device by turning it off and back on again is similar to what play does to an overwhelmed brain. Wendy Mason, director of early learning at an independent school in Melbourne, sees the consequences of children not having enough time to play. 'More children than ever [are] arriving at school with decreased ability to concentrate, the inability to focus and listen and [have] difficulty articulating their emotions . . . and having an underdeveloped imagination.'[5]

Through free play your daughter will have the opportunity to get to know herself better – what she likes, what she doesn't, what she's naturally good at, and what takes more effort. She can try different activities without being measured or feeling the pressure to perform, and she can role-play different personas. It's one reason why Lea Waters, psychology professor at the University of Melbourne, encourages parents to 'fearlessly feature downtime' in children's schedules. 'They're sorting through what they've taken in, attaching emotional meaning to it, cementing it in memory, integrating it into their core selves. It's all part of building their identity, about learning who they are apart from what they do,' Waters writes in *The Strength Switch*.[6]

The freedom to experiment and explore will increase the chances of your daughter finding her passion – the pursuit that makes her heart sing, what she was born to do. Some adults go their whole lives without ever discovering their passion, and yet it is critical to mental health. A passion can bring meaning and purpose to an otherwise mundane life. Some people are lucky enough to know immediately what they were born to do, but most people have to search for it and work at it. Play is an opportunity for your daughter to begin that process.

By allowing our girls to play, we will be achieving many of the objectives that we set out to achieve with structured learning programs – without the stress that comes with an over-scheduled childhood. And, better still, this kind of play is free (or low cost). Remember, by play we mean spontaneous, child-led activities that are not outcome-focused. Play is when a girl unselfconsciously dances around her bedroom as opposed to going to a ballet lesson. It's when she swings on the monkey bars rather than going to gym class, or when she sings into her hairbrush instead of practising scales with a singing instructor. Often children's weeks are so tightly scheduled there is not a single moment where they are free from adult instruction or outcome-based activities. This is not a childhood. It's boot camp.

How to take back free time

Carving out free time can be hard. No, scratch that: it *is* hard.

Due to our daughters' pester power of wanting to do the same extracurricular activities as their friends and, if we're really honest, some deep-seated parenting anxiety and fear about our girls missing out, we reached a point where they were busy every afternoon and evening after school and preschool. They were either in after-school care or long day care (on the days we were working) or at an extracurricular activity. We realised that if we wanted our girls to get the time to play that they needed then we were going to have to make a conscious effort to schedule it into our family life.

So we made a rule: other than weekly swimming lessons, we allowed our girls to choose *one* extracurricular activity that they could do on the weekend. Now on our free weekday afternoons, instead of rushing to an activity, when the weather is fine one of us will take them to the park instead. It takes exactly the same time commitment from us, with the added bonus of being free. Often there are other children at the park to play with, but sometimes there aren't and the girls have to find ways to entertain themselves. When the weather is wet we take them to the library, or some days we'll go straight home and the girls will draw, play Lego or build a world in Minecraft. Yes, we are endorsing 'slacker parenting'. Embrace it.

Aren't we concerned that cutting out their activities will lead to a life of obesity? The short answer is no.

Children don't have to be at a structured, adult-led, competitive activity in order to exercise. Over the course of a week, our girls are moving their bodies just as much as they did before. Plus they get the added benefit of being outside and having free and spontaneous play, which enhances their physical, emotional and spiritual wellbeing.

We understand that it is a privilege for us to be able to spend time with our girls in the afternoons, and that not all families can do this. But there may be other ways you can shift the balance so your daughter can get more activity from play and less from structured learning. Opt for an after-school care service that is play-based, rather than sending her to a structured lesson. Or team up with other parents and have rotating playdates after school or preschool. Another option is to reserve time on the weekend that is explicitly for play, and to treat that time like a serious commitment so that it doesn't get eaten away by other priorities. When spare time pops up in your family schedule, fill it with play.

It is also worth remembering that when it comes to obesity, exercise is only one contributing factor. Other factors are stress, lack of sleep and, of course, poor eating habits. All three of these can occur as a result of over-scheduling kids.

Do our girls nag us to watch TV instead of play? Yes! Do we allow them to? More often than we'd like to admit. Do they complain when we don't let them? Absolutely! But after the protests and moaning have died down, the girls will often go into their bedroom and find something else to do. Sometimes it is reading, other times it's playing with Lego, or making boats and trains for their toys out of the boxes in the recycling bin.

And, full disclosure, there are times when our girls tell us that they are bored. There was a period of adjustment when they had to learn how to play. They were so used to being entertained, they didn't know how to entertain themselves. We even borrowed a book from the library called *Today We Have No Plans*, by Jane Godwin and Anna Walker, to get the girls used to the idea of doing nothing. (Yes, we agree that it's bizarre to get a book out of the library to learn about free time, but the concept really was that novel to them!)

We clearly weren't the only family unfamiliar with the concept of free time. According to the IKEA report mentioned previously, free time is so unfamiliar to families that, when they do get it, they don't know what to do with it. Half of all kids and parents admitted that they'd have to stop and think about how to spend an extra couple of hours of free time. Not only do we not know what to do with free time, we are so out of practice that the very idea of it is stressful. Fifty-three per cent of kids and 46 per cent of adults surveyed said they are anxious when presented with free time, with unplanned time giving rise to unpleasant feelings of chaos and loss of control.

But despite free time being outside our collective comfort zone, it's exactly what we crave. Sixty-six per cent of kids and

73 per cent of adults agree that the best family times are unplanned. A whopping 89 per cent of kids aged 6–11 years said they wish they had more time to spend with family. Kids are so keen to just hang out with their parents that they even claim they would be happy to do tasks they don't particularly like in order to achieve this – even chores!

Our decision to prioritise play in our girls' lives has had profound and enduring benefits. They are both noticeably calmer. And you know what? So are we. Admittedly, our not having structured activities during the week might strike some as extreme. It works for us but it may not work for you. But if your daughter's extracurricular activities add stress to your family life or cut into her time to play, then it might be worth considering if you've got the balance right. Perhaps you could get your daughter to drop just one activity so you have an extra afternoon a week when you're not rushing to be somewhere, when your daughter can play freely and experience flow and calm.

The tutoring arms race

You might be on board with the importance of play. And you may agree that extracurricular activities such as dance, tribal drumming or theatre can be dropped. But what about academic extracurricular activities like tutoring? Aren't they good for kids? A lot of parents think so. In fact, Australian Tutoring Association chief executive Mohan Dhall estimates the number of students being tutored is as high as one in seven.[7]

When we were school-aged, tutoring was the exception. It was for kids who had missed a lot of school because they'd been sick, or in hospital, and needed to catch up. Or it was for kids who had specific learning difficulties and needed special help in a particular area.

Not anymore: tutoring has become commonplace. And it's not just that more children are enrolled in tutoring; there has also been an explosion in the kinds of subjects kids can be tutored for. There is a tutoring service for every occasion, from 'school readiness' tutoring for kids who are almost still in nappies, to exam preparation tutoring for NAPLAN, selective entry school exams and Year 12 exams. Then there is the everyday tutoring to make sure your kid gets to take home readers from the advanced box, or is among the first in her class to recite her times tables. While there may be occasions when some children need help with a specific area of learning, the expansion of tutoring suggests that it is no longer about ensuring children don't fall behind. Rather, it seems to be about getting ahead of the next kid.

Tanith Carey, author of *Taming the Tiger Parent*, says the increase in the number of children undertaking tutoring, and its broadening into a whole range of areas, feeds on parents' fears about their children getting left behind. Parents see other parents enrolling their kids in tutoring so they feel that they should too, and before they know it, they are coughing up their hard-earned cash and their children are being over-scheduled.[8] In short, parents and their children have been recruited, often unwittingly and for the best of intentions, into an arms race of achievement.

Does tutoring actually work?

The appeal of tutoring is easy enough to grasp. After all, if some education is good, then more must be better, right? But if you step back and look at the evidence for the effectiveness of tutoring, the 'more is better' approach doesn't really hold up. The best that can be said for tutoring is that it provides limited benefits. At worst, it can be detrimental to a child's education.

Judith Ireson and Katie Rushforth, researchers from the University of London's Institute of Education, looked at exam results for 3515 children aged 11, 16 and 18 and discovered that tutored kids didn't perform much better than their untutored peers. Those who had received private tutoring scored less than half a grade higher in their maths exams, with the benefit for girls being even smaller than it was for boys. The difference in the test results for English between those who received tutoring and those who didn't was negligible.[9]

Let's just think about that for a moment. Thousands of dollars and precious hours for zilch, nada and diddly squat.

Dr Pearl Subban, who researches in Educational Psychology and Inclusive Education at Monash University, says that one of the reasons tutoring doesn't bring the hoped-for outcomes is that it can make children reliant on the tutor and thereby rob them of the ability to develop the vital skills of self-directed learning and initiative. 'I'm not going to say that tutoring is bad; I'm sure that it's providing a service and fulfilling a need,' says Dr Subban. 'But at the same time, there must be an awareness of increasing the child's independence, not increasing dependency on a tutor.'

Dr Subban cautions parents to think about the effect that tutoring can have on their child's overall wellbeing. 'Tutoring can increase stress and pressure on students. It makes the child think that they have to perform really well all the time, that the numbers matter. That there's no room for someone who's mediocre and middle of the road,' she says. 'Students become really worn out by working very hard. The tutoring sessions are often held after school hours, sometimes on a weekend and, as a result, students are given little free time, and the school/life balance becomes askew.'

Forcing your daughter to do too much academic work before she is ready or when she is tired and stressed could backfire. Instead of advancing her learning, you could turn her into a child who hates learning. We've seen this firsthand. One of Violet's friends started Kumon lessons when she was a toddler. Her parents were persuaded by the claims that they would be giving their daughter a head start if she could read before she started school. They handed over thousands of dollars and had countless arguments with their young daughter, who would have preferred to be doing pretty much anything other than literacy lessons. In the end this little girl was able to read before she started school. So far so good.

By the end of the first year of school, most of the kids in Violet's grade were reading at the same level. But there was one distinct difference. The little girl who had been tutored hated reading because it was work. Her parents told us that it was a struggle to get her to read anything. Now, it may be that she's just not much interested in reading. Perhaps the tutoring made her a better reader than she might otherwise have been. We'll never know. One thing that is certain is that tutoring did nothing to inspire a love of reading. In fact, it achieved just the opposite. The outcome of those Kumon lessons was buckets of tears and a girl who will only read when there's an adult standing over her telling her that she has to.

We're not suggesting that this is going to be the experience for every child. Your daughter may take to these classes like a duck to water. To be sure, there are some cases where tutoring can be beneficial. But we need to be careful not to get sucked into the tutoring frenzy, because it not only may fail to deliver the academic benefits you are expecting, but also could add to your daughter's stress and affect her sense of calm.

Homework: if it were a student, it would get an F

Something similar applies to homework. While less intensive than tutoring, homework is another one of those activities that we think must improve academic performance. But its imagined benefits are just that: imaginary. The research doesn't support homework, especially for young children. It may benefit adolescents in the secondary years, but as Mike Horsley and Richard Walker write in *Reforming Homework*, 'Homework has no achievement benefits for students up to grade 3 [and] negligible benefits for students in grades 4–6.'[10]

Let us repeat that for emphasis. Walker and Horsley spent two years examining data from around the world and found that primary-school children derived little to no academic benefit from homework.

Parenting author and former teacher Maggie Dent calls herself the 'anti-homework queen': she says that homework is a waste of time and the last thing children need after an exhausting day at school. 'There is no research to show that homework in primary school improves school performance,' Dent says. 'And as for parents who do their kid's homework for them – how is that going to help them when they do the next in-class assessment? Children especially need to be playing with other children or their parents and relaxing, getting ready for the next day's schooling!'[11]

Despite the overwhelming research showing that homework for young kids does not deliver the academic benefits we might imagine, parents often demand it from schools. Some parents insist their kids do even more work by setting their own homework and taking kids to private maths and English classes.

Maggie Dent knows of four-year-old children who have been set an hour and a half of homework. 'They have to go home and colour within the lines,' says Dent, who asserts that many children lack the fine motor skills to successfully complete the task. 'That horrifies me. You're asking children to do something that they're actually not developmentally able to do. And you're asking them to do it over and over again.'

Even for students in later years, there is only a correlation between doing homework and academic success. Correlation is not causation. It may be that students who do more homework are more motivated anyway: more motivation probably means a greater chance of both conscientiously completed homework and good grades. As Horsley and Walker write, 'It is individual students themselves who will ultimately decide what they will learn from homework.'[12]

Of course, some will point to other benefits of homework, aside from the alleged academic benefits. It's often claimed that homework teaches kids time management and study skills while instilling good work habits. But there's little evidence to show that's the case. US education expert Alfie Kohn writes in *The Homework Myth* that homework may do this, or it may not. The fact is no one knows as the research hasn't been done. But he's doubtful that the supposed benefits would occur in practice.

Take time management as an example. In theory homework should instil time management skills. But if parents are the ones who are reminding their child to do their homework and ensuring it's completed and submitted on time, then it's the parents who are managing the time, not the child. Kohn writes that 'one mother remarked that her kids' assignments are really testing *her* proficiency at time management'.[13] While Kohn says that the answer might be to allow your child to flounder and fail, that's unlikely to work in the long term. 'The consequences are unpleasant for parent and child alike if the assignment is discovered undone just before bedtime or early the next morning. In fact, if it remains undone, parents can usually count on hearing from the teacher, which would suggest that a hands-off policy on the part of parents really isn't expected or desired.'[14]

At the other end of the spectrum, there are kids who waste too much time needlessly obsessing over their homework. 'What the teacher sees is a complete piece of work, but they don't know what's gone down at home,' says Dent. 'Some kids take two hours to do what is a set piece of twenty minutes. And then we have perfection-driven children who do the task over and over and over again, to an unhealthy level.'

Another common argument in favour of homework is that it teaches kids discipline, that they don't always get to do what they want in life. But children spend all day at school following other people's rules, doing things that they didn't choose to do. What's so wrong with them being able to do what they want with their time at home? It's called 'free time' for a reason. Adults don't want to bring their work home with them each night, so it seems bizarre to expect that kids should be any different.

That's not to say that children learn nothing from homework. On the contrary, many learn to loathe any kind of formal learning. It can also teach kids that there is no downtime. To quote Associate Professor Tara Magdalinski, Dean of Learning Innovation at Swinburne University of Technology's Faculty of Health, Arts and Design, 'I think homework teaches students something else – how not to respect work/life boundaries.'

It also creates tension in households. As Tanith Carey writes, 'Homework has a tendency to turn your home into a war zone. Surveys have found that homework is the single biggest source of friction between children and parents. One survey found that 40 per cent of kids say they have cried during a row over it. Even that figure seems like an underestimate.'

If homework is turning your home into a war zone, Maggie Dent recommends having a respectful conversation with your daughter's school about what you feel is best for your daughter and your family. For example, if you decide that one day a week you are going to have a quiet afternoon with your daughter and play longer at the park, politely explain to the teacher that your daughter will not be able to do homework on that particular day.

The one exception to the hands-off homework policy

The one exception we have to homework is reading. Setting aside time each night to read to your daughter is the kind of 'homework' that should be encouraged. This might involve reading to her just before she goes to bed or, when she's old enough, making time for her to read to you, and also encouraging her to read on her own. When your daughter becomes a competent reader, there are benefits to continuing to read aloud to her – even as she enters her tweens and teenage years. Some parents make the mistake of thinking that once their child has learned to read, and those gawd-awful readers stop coming home each night, their job is done and they no longer need to focus on reading. But there are so many benefits to continuing to read together in the home well beyond the point where children can read for themselves.

Dr Alice Sullivan, Professor of Sociology at the Institute of Education, University College London, found that children who read books regularly at ten years of age, and more than once a week at sixteen years of age, performed better at school. As Dr Sullivan said in an article published in the *Telegraph*, 'It may seem surprising that reading for pleasure would help to improve children's maths scores. But it is likely that strong reading ability will enable children to absorb and understand new information and affect their attainment in all subjects.'[15]

Arguably, even more important than academic performance, you should encourage your daughter to be a reader because readers have better mental health and healthier relationships.[16] Reading can also expose your daughter to a greater number and range of words than she might hear in daily life. Time spent together reading can establish a lifelong love of books and can be a good bonding activity. It's also a great way for her to wind down and get ready for sleep.

But – and this is crucial – you must allow your daughter to choose the books she reads. If she wants to dip into comics or graphic novels, let her. If she wants to read stories about unicorns and fairies that you consider 'childish' and that she should have moved beyond, let her. Some parents are concerned with making sure their children are only reading the readers set by the school, or with finding 'quality' books that have won literary awards. However, if she's not interested in these kinds of materials, this approach is likely to alienate your daughter and turn her off reading altogether. After all, *you* wouldn't spend time reading books that you hate. And it's a fair bet that your daughter feels the same way. Kohn writes, 'Nothing contributes to a student's interest in (and proficiency at) reading more than the opportunity to read books that he or she has chosen.'[17]

When Violet started to read, the school gave her readers to bring home each night. These were great to begin with, as they were at the right level. But as she grew more competent, she also grew bored with them. She wanted to read other books. While she continued to bring readers home, we'd leave the reader in her bag and allow her to read whatever she wanted. We didn't just want Violet to learn the mechanics of reading. We wanted her to learn to love reading, and we feared that if we forced her to read books that didn't excite her we would jeopardise that goal. It's no fun for a child – or their parents – to wade through books that they have no interest in reading. Instead, be guided by your daughter's curiosity and passions so she's more likely to *want* to read.

When Violet was going through her unicorn phase we borrowed every unicorn book in our local library. When her interests shifted onto dogs we did the same. This included non-fiction books on dog breeds and dog care. When we saw articles in newspapers about dogs we sat down and read them with her too. Story books, factual books, comics, magazine or newspaper articles: it doesn't matter. If your daughter is reading, then that's your job done. It's not (another) activity that you need to assign, design and structure. To instil a love of reading, treat it like play: make it child-led.

Get caught reading

Bickering, dropping the F-bomb, eating our children's Easter eggs on the sly: these are just some of the things that parents hope never to be sprung doing in front of their kids. But there's one activity we should definitely go out of our way to get caught doing: reading.

We're not talking about reading to your kids. We're talking about reading for yourself. And not just any old reading. It has to be reading for pleasure, so this is unlikely to include functional reading like scanning the school news-letter or the manual for the new washing machine. It means sitting down and reading for the pure fun of it.

According to children's literacy expert Joy Bandy, one of the very best things you can do for your children is to model the joy of reading. 'Make the process of reading appear exciting and mysterious to children,' says Bandy. 'If children interrupt, you say, "Excuse me, I just want to finish this chapter. It's so exciting I want to find out what happens."'

Bandy, who is now a grandmother, says that parents should make an effort to 'get caught' reading anything that they and the child are interested in, such as comics, newspaper articles, and even cricket scores. 'With my grandchildren I will open the newspaper and say, "Have you seen this comic strip? What do you think of it?"'

We know what you're thinking. When are you going to find time to model reading for the sheer pleasure of it? It's just another task to add to the long list of things 'good parents' are supposed to do. But as we've already discussed, many parents invest an enormous amount of time and money in out-of-school activities. Dropping just one extra-curricular activity could open up the time to visit the library once a week instead.

That's what the mother of British comedian and mega-successful children's author David Walliams did. Walliams describes himself as a previously reluctant reader. 'I much preferred watching TV,' he said to a packed stadium of young fans in Melbourne for the launch of his book *Bad Dad*. Despite his lack of interest in books, his mother took him to the library every week. And then one week, when he was twelve years old, he picked up *Charlie and the Chocolate Factory*. He fell in love with the book, and subsequently fell in love with reading.

'I think that adults who say that they don't like reading, it's because they never got to find as a child that one book they loved and couldn't put down,' said Walliams.

While not every child is going to grow up to be a best-selling celebrity author and comic, providing our children with the opportunity to develop a love of reading is giving them the gift of imagination, entertainment, empathy and improved academic performance. Taking a bit of 'me time' with a book is great for you and your kids.

The great screen debate

Most parents love the idea of their children reading books. But this wasn't always the case. Back in the early eighteenth century, when books became more affordable and more people began reading them, there was much hand-wringing about the damage they might do to young and impressionable minds. In particular, critics wondered whether novels would lead people – mostly women – to be unable to differentiate between real and made-up worlds.[18] This seems strange to us now. No one nowadays argues that books are anything but great.

Screens, on the other hand, are the modern-day bogeyman. Many parents react to the presence of a screen near children, particularly young children, as if it's poison. Parents have told us that they feel under pressure to enrol their girls in extracurricular activities because of screen time. If her free time is booked up with activities, so the logic goes, she won't be on a screen. Allowing their child to use a screen often tops the list of things parents feel guilty about.

That's not surprising given that health authorities and the media are full of horror stories about screens. We're told that screens are making kids fatter and dumber, and stunting their emotional development. There are also claims that internet use is changing the structures of children's brains, with some linking more screen time to increases in autism and ADHD.[19]

The American Academy of Pediatrics (AAP) recommends limiting screen use to one hour per day for 2–5-year-olds and no screen time for children under two years except for chatting with grandparents, for example.[20] This advice is echoed by the Sydney Children's Hospitals Network (although they allow one to two hours of screen time for 2–5-year-olds) and the Mayo Clinic in the United States.[21] The World Health Organization (WHO) similarly recommends no sedentary screen time for children under one year of age and no more than one hour per day for two-year-olds.[22] The WHO adds that 'less is better', pointing to links between the time children sit in front of screens and excess fat, delayed motor and cognitive development, and poor emotional health.

A warning like that is enough to scare any parent and induce a torrent of guilt when their child does inevitably look at a screen.

But here's the thing: the studies pointing out the dire effects of screen time on kids aren't as solid as they may at first appear. The truth is, the evidence for screen time being bad for kids is pretty flimsy.

Take, for example, the WHO's recommendations. They say their recommendations are based on systematic reviews of data published in peer-reviewed journals on the relationship between physical activity, sedentary behaviour (specifically sedentary behaviour reported by parents as passive screen use), sleep and various health outcomes. All of this sounds impressive – until you read the accompanying commentary the WHO provides on the quality of evidence. In the same report where the WHO makes its recommendations, it also admits they are 'strong recommendations [based on] very low-quality evidence'. The WHO goes on to acknowledge that its recommendations on the links between screen time and body fat, cognitive and motor skills development and psychosocial health are based on 'moderate to very low-quality evidence' and that 'the overall quality of evidence was rated as very low'.

Similarly, the studies on which the AAP bases its guidelines don't always make a clear connection between screen time and the various ills it reportedly produces. For example, one of the AAP's papers on the links between watching TV and obesity says that the connection is explained by kids watching junk-food advertising, rather than watching media. As the authors note, 'It is believed that exposure to food advertising and watching television while eating (which diminishes attention to satiety cues) drives these associations.'[23] Presumably, this association is reduced if your child is watching ABC Kids or playing Minecraft.

Another study that the AAP uses looked at the effect of television viewing on children's 'executive function' (EF). This refers to children's capacity to stick at and achieve goals, which has obvious benefits for how kids perform in school. The study looked at what kids watched and found that watching educational programs, such as those on the US's Public Broadcasting Service, 'was associated with better EF performance, whereas viewing of educational cartoons was related to worse EF performance'.[24] So, firstly, what kids are watching matters. The authors also conceded that 'we do not know whether the relation between television viewing and EF is causal or not'.[25] In other words, the researchers couldn't tell you whether watching TV reduces executive function or whether kids with lower executive function are more likely to watch TV. This study wasn't able to confirm either theory.

Untangling causal relationships between screens and development is one of the biggest challenges of making definitive claims about technology and health. One of the problems with the research, says Dr Amy Orben from the University of Oxford's Department of Experimental Psychology, is it often mistakes correlation for causality. 'It's the same kind of thing with murder rates going up when ice cream sales go up. There's no relation between the two, but murder rates are higher in the summer and ice cream sales are also higher in the summer,' says Dr Orben, who has looked at the effects of screen use on teenage kids. Similarly, the wide availability of screens and increasing reports of anxiety and depression and other health problems among kids have occurred together, but no causal link has been proven.

Another problem is that the researchers who look at these issues sift through mountains of data before making their claims. While that makes their findings more robust, because they're based on lots of data, it also means that what might otherwise be tiny effects take on a significance that might go unnoticed in everyday life. Dr Orben says children would need to use screens for up to eleven hours per day or more to experience a decrease in wellbeing. And while we've all heard stories of kids 'addicted' to video games, they are the exception rather than the rule.

Dr Orben illustrates this point with the example of wearing glasses. 'If a teenager wears glasses to school, that also has a negative correlation with their wellbeing. That correlation is also really, really small. It is statistically significant – and it's actually larger than the one between digital technologies and wellbeing.' Yes, that's right: according to the evidence, when it comes to wellbeing, wearing glasses is actually worse for kids than using social media. Of course, no one's suggesting that children shouldn't wear glasses just because of a small – though statistically significant – decline in wellbeing. The same thinking should apply to screens.

And what about the supposed link between screen time and autism and ADHD? This one is completely false. There is no such link. In fact, one of the most vocal people asserting a link between screen use and autism, Baroness Susan Greenfield, has been publicly asked to stop repeating baseless claims about the effects of screen time on kids' brains. Professor of Developmental Neuropsychology Dorothy Bishop published an open letter to Greenfield, saying, 'I wish you would focus on communicating about your areas of expertise . . . But please, please, stop talking about autism.'[26]

These problems with the quality of evidence for the dangers of screen time is one reason that the Royal College of Paediatrics and Child Health (RCPCH) in the United Kingdom, unlike their colleagues in Australia and the United States, doesn't publish strict guidelines on screen time for kids. As the RCPCH explains: 'There is not enough evidence to confirm that screen time is in itself harmful to child health at any age, making it impossible to recommend age-appropriate time limits.' Instead, the RCPCH suggests 'that parents approach screen time based on the child's developmental age, the individual need and value the family place on positive activities such as socialising, exercise and sleep – when screen time displaces these activities, the evidence suggests there is a risk to child wellbeing'.[27]

What to do about screens?

We are not advocating that kids become couch potatoes, whiling away their hours glued to screens. We are also not suggesting that there are no adverse effects of screen time and technology. We've all heard of kids who can't tear themselves away from screens, and there are legitimate concerns about tech companies that use their massive wealth and resources to design their apps and services to hook users – both children and adults – for as long as possible. There is also cyberbullying and stories about kids being contacted and groomed by strangers on apps or through the chat functions of games. There are also legitimate concerns about privacy and other online safety issues. Further, we think that many of the claims about educational apps should be treated with a healthy dose of scepticism.

But these are not problems of screens, technology or the internet per se. These are problems for parents – and ones that are within our control. Know that you have the power and the right to manage your child's screen time. Read up on safety, lock down devices and manage the privacy controls and the restrictions on apps. A good place to start gathering this knowledge is the website of Australia's eSafety Commissioner, which has heaps of information about keeping kids safe online.[28]

Make sure that your daughter is using devices in areas where you can see her and intervene if she receives messages or content that are inappropriate. In our family we have a 'no iPad in the bedroom' rule. Unless there is a special circumstance, when our daughters are on screens they must be in the lounge room, where we can monitor what they are doing.

Sydney-based registered psychologist Jocelyn Brewer recommends that parents work out a 'digital diet' for their families, rather than just saying no to screens. 'We really need to empower parents to help them work out what their digital diet and the digital menu look like for their family, and how does that fit into bigger questions of when do you go and spend time in the outdoors or as a family, and how and when do you eat meals, and all of that other contextual wellbeing.' If your daughter's screen time fits in with your family, and she's doing what she needs to in school and in her personal life, then allowing her to spend some of her downtime using a screen won't turn her into a mindless zombie.

You might be wondering what screens have to do with creating a sense of calm for your daughter. We have seen a link between screen use paranoia and over-scheduling. We know parents who have booked their children into activities late into the evening every single day because they fear that if their children are at home they will be on their screens the whole time. If this is also your fear, then know this: while the evidence that screen use harms children is weak to non-existent, the evidence that sleep-deprivation, anxiety and stress harm children is very strong. If you are keeping your daughter super busy because of a fear of screens, it might be time for a rethink.

Sleep

Many of the decisions we make as parents are yet to be tested. We do the best we can with the information we have, but only time will tell if we've got it right. It's therefore comforting to know that there is one part of your parenting strategy you can know with absolute certainty you're getting right: sleep.

Get sleep right, and everything works better. We mean *everything*. As neuroscientist Dr Sarah McKay writes in *The Women's Brain Book*, 'No aspect of our biology is safe from sleep deprivation. Skip one night's sleep and you will feel utterly dreadful. Suffer from insomnia regularly, get insufficient sleep . . . and you're at risk of depression, metabolic disorders such as type 2 diabetes, cardio-vascular disease, cognitive decline and a host of other problems, including increased mortality.'[29]

The current evidence suggests that young children in Australia get enough sleep. The Australian Institute of Family Studies reports that most Australian 6–7-year-olds are getting enough sleep during the week, with most boys and girls going to bed at around 8 pm. What is enough, and is your daughter getting it? According to the National Sleep Foundation, primary-school children need between 9 and 11 hours per night and secondary-school children need between 8 and 10 hours.

How much sleep should your daughter be getting?

Age	Recommended	May be appropriate	Not recommended
Toddlers 1–2 years	11–14 hours	9–10 hours 15–16 hours	Less than 9 hours More than 16 hours
Preschoolers 3–5 years	10–13 hours	8–9 hours 14 hours	Less than 8 hours More than 14 hours
Primary schoolers 6–13 years	9–11 hours	7–8 hours 12 hours	Less than 7 hours More than 12 hours

Source: The Sleep Health Foundation

Some kids are naturally better sleepers than others and, of course, throughout life there are going to be factors that affect sleep quality from time to time. But in general, good sleep is a skill your daughter can practise and learn, just like any other skill.

Our girls weren't sleepers. In fact, they were so bad that we ended up at sleep school for both of them. This turned out to be a blessing because the team of nurses, doctors and psychologists there taught us to prioritise sleep and consistent sleep routines. There was no magic here, by the way. In our case, at least, turning our girls into sleepers was all about creating the right conditions for them to sleep, and prioritising those conditions above all else.

As kids get older, there is a temptation to sacrifice sleep for other activities. Extracurricular activities can start before school and stretch into the evening, meaning that children get to bed later and wake earlier. Or children don't get enough downtime in the evenings, so they go to bed wired and unable to fall asleep.

Sacrificing our children's sleep is, in part, driven by the competitive nature of our society. Dr Sarah Blunden, psychologist and director of the Australian Centre for Education in Sleep, says she and her colleagues – including teachers, researchers and clinicians – have seen a shift in our expectations of kids:

> We think that young people at school do have a lot more on their plate than they used to have. There is a lot more competition; we're a competitive country, and we tend to push them harder and harder. Even though sleep is getting a bit of a better profile these days, we do give up sleep for things that we find 'better for us': better for our future, better for our intellect, better for our development and learning.

But the costs of our competitiveness and over-scheduling – and our daughters' subsequent growing sleep debts – may not be worth it in the long run. Tired girls struggle to concentrate and learn. Tired girls have trouble regulating their emotions. Tired girls are risking their physical and mental health. Is any extracurricular activity or learning opportunity really worth that?

Trying to make sure a girl reaches her full potential by loading her schedule with extracurricular activities that eat into her sleep time is simply not worth it. That includes social activities or too much homework. You can't expect your daughter to rush from school to basketball to tutoring, get home at 7 pm, eat her dinner, do her homework, tell you about her day, and then be calm enough to fall asleep by 8 pm. Something has to give. And that something shouldn't be sleep.

The good news is that if your daughter is a poor sleeper, this can be fixed. 'The great thing about sleep is that sleep is modifiable,' says Dr Blunden. She suggests making small changes, such as adjusting your daughter's bedtime and wake-time by 15 minutes every 2–3 days. When they've adjusted to the new times, move them by 15 minutes again, until they're getting the right amount of sleep.

Our daughters' non-negotiable bedtime routines include wind-down time: bath, teeth, reading, toilet, bed. Since Violet started school we have allowed her a window of quiet time for silent reading or colouring in her bed before lights out. Crucially, this time does not involve screens, as the blue light from phones and iPads makes our brains think it's daytime. We learned this the hard way. When screens crept into Violet's bedtime routine she would lie in bed wide awake and wired at 10 pm. Now that we don't let our girls look at screens one hour before bed, they mostly fall asleep when their heads hit the pillow.

And when it's bedtime, our girls go to bed. If they come out – assuming they're not sick or having a nightmare – they are turned around and told to go back to bed. They have the odd later night for a special occasion, but when we say 'odd', we mean two or three times a year. Otherwise, bedtime is the same every night. No exceptions.

We have been told more times than we can count that we are

too inflexible when it comes to our girls' sleep. But for us it is worth it because we rarely have tired children. As every parent knows, everything is harder when children are tired. Our strict bedtime routine makes life so much easier and happier for everyone in our family.

Action for dads

Take your daughter to your local library.

Libraries are wonderful. They're a haven in your and your daughter's busy lives where you can slow down and be calm together. They're also an opportunity for you to model reading for pleasure to your daughter. Pick up a book, sit down and start reading and encourage your daughter to do the same. She can read next to you or you can read the same book together.

You don't like books? That's okay. If you haven't been into a library in a while, you may discover that they have changed since you were in knee-high socks. Local libraries are chock-full of DVDs, CDs, computer games, magazines and newspapers. Many subscribe to streaming services for film, music, ebooks and audio-books. Even when the library is closed, it's open.

Pretty much all the blockbuster books, movies and music are held by your library. And if you can't find what you like, many libraries have online forms where you can recommend purchases. If their suppliers can get it, and it fits within their collection guide-lines and budget, we've found that they usually purchase it.

The best way to encourage your daughter to become a reader is to find books that she's interested in. When in doubt, ask a librarian. (That should be on a t-shirt.) We promise that if your daughter walks up to a librarian and asks for help to find a book on her favourite subject, she will make that librarian's day. Your daughter will also have practised the skill of speaking for herself, adding to her sense of independence and mastery. (We'll cover this more in the next chapter.)

When your daughter is older, get her a library card and watch her face light up with joy and pride when she uses it. There is something about having a card that will make her feel that she now has a personal stake in the library. She'll belong to the not-so-secret club of readers.

Going to the library together won't just give your daughter a sense of calm and connection when she is young. It can become a cherished ritual that you can do together your whole lives.

Recap

- Parenting can feel like a never-ending to-do list. There is always something extra you feel you should be doing to maximise your daughter's potential. The good news is that you can opt out of some of it. The quest to constantly push our daughters to be smarter, stronger, fitter, faster and more productive is one ride you and your daughter can – and definitely should – get off. As counterintuitive as it may sound, raising a girl who likes herself can mean doing less, rather than more.

- Parents often prioritise enhancement activities while squeezing play and sleep into the cracks. Play and sleep are first to go when times are busy, but it should be the other way around. To raise a girl who likes herself, play and sleep must be a priority. Then enhancement activities can be slotted in *only* if and when there is free time.

- It can take a lot to push back against the extracurricular activities frenzy, the tutoring arms race and overblown fear of screens. But think back to why you picked up our book. Was it because you want to raise a girl who gets into Mensa? Was it to raise a girl who will win a stream of awards and accolades that you can post on Facebook to make your friends envious? Unlikely. We're betting that you want to raise a girl who likes herself. And a girl who likes herself is calm.

5

A girl who likes herself is independent and masterful

Do you remember the first time you rode a bike on your own? Perhaps you don't recall the exact time or day, but you probably remember the emotion. The feeling of propelling yourself under your own steam, of finally getting the hang of it, legs working in harmony with the cranks, keeping balanced while managing to steer is a defining moment in childhood. We talk about it, reminisce about it, record it.

Why is bike riding such a momentous event in a child's life? One reason is that not only is it hard to do, it is something that a child must do all on their own. While parents can encourage and help them to get their balance, bike riding is something that every child must do by themselves. For many children it is likely one of the first times that they are old enough to remember having a sense of mastery, of doing something by themselves that comes after a period of struggle, frustration, failure, persistence, and then success.

The bliss, pride and empowerment that a girl feels when she first rides a bike on her own cannot be replicated by anything we do for her, say to her, or give her. You can't manufacture that experience or buy it in a bottle. You can't give the life-affirming satisfaction of mastery to someone else. It can only be experienced firsthand. This feeling is the essence of life, these moments are what we live for. And they cannot occur without parents giving their children the gift of frustration and failure.

Yes, frustration and failure are a gift, but one we parents often find difficult to give. Watching our children experience frustration and failure is painful. It seems to go against our instincts as parents, and there is an awful lot of social pressure for parents to create the 'perfect' childhood for their daughters that minimises frustration and failure.

When we first became parents we assumed it was our job to give our girls an easy ride on the back of our bikes. But now we know different. One of our most important responsibilities is to support and encourage our girls to develop their independence and mastery so they can ride their own bike in every aspect of their lives. This is the key to building self-esteem. Parents can tell their daughter how great she is until they are blue in the face but it will not make her like herself. Liking yourself blooms from within and it grows from the fertile soil of mastery.

In this chapter we are going to outline the case for allowing your daughter to develop mastery and independence and give you some evidence-based strategies to help her do this. But first, let's start with a story.

Feel-good parenting

Five-year-old Elly is sitting up at the kitchen table with her cousin, twelve-year-old Jessica. Jessica has been learning about portrait painting in her art class at school, so the girls decide to paint portraits of Elly's Emma Wiggle doll. Emma Wiggle is propped up at the end of the table, with her huge sparkly eyes and dressed in her trademark yellow and black bows and little ballet shoes. Elly's dad is hovering, occasionally looking over to make sure the jars of water don't get knocked over and paint doesn't get splattered on the wall from overenthusiastic brush strokes.

Ten minutes pass and Jessica's portrait is looking good. She's done a great job of capturing the Emma doll's likeness. Elly's portrait, meanwhile, looks like a cross between a yellow and black oil slick and roadkill – exactly what you'd expect a five-year-old to produce.

Little Elly compares the two paintings and her shoulders slump. 'Mine is bad. I'm stupid,' she says.

Her dad is a child of the 1980s. Along with big hair, acid-wash jeans and He-Man, he grew up in the midst of the self-esteem movement. This hinged on the idea that self-esteem is the magic key to unlocking the kingdom of happiness and success. All parents and teachers had to do to give children the self-esteem key was chant the magic words 'You are great' – or variations of this – often enough.

If your childhood was anything like ours, you would have been the recipient of numerous 'feeling good' campaigns at school. There may have been posters in your classroom or you may have been given workbooks that squealed 'You are special', 'Everybody loves you' and 'You can do anything'. Some teachers stopped marking tests with a red pen because this colour was supposed to damage self-esteem. It was as if making a mistake was so disastrous for a child that their teacher needed to soften the blow.

'Your painting is great,' Dad assures Elly, as all those lessons from his own childhood kick in. 'It's so good it should be in an art gallery. You are a great artist.'

In response, Elly scrunches up her painting in frustration. 'No, it isn't. Jessica's painting is good. Mine looks like a poo.' Tears are brewing in her sweet little eyes.

'Don't worry, honey, I'll paint Emma doll for you,' says Dad, undeterred. He whips up a quick portrait of Emma. He's no artist but it's quite good, even if he does say so himself.

Dad is feeling pretty good about himself at this point. As for Elly, not so much.

The problem with 'You are awesome!' parenting

The self-esteem movement casts a long shadow. Spend five minutes in any playground and listen to all the unearned praise (and often outright lies) of 'Great job!' and 'You are so awesome!' coming out of parents' mouths.

We feel good making these comments to our kids. We feel even better when it provokes a smile out of them. But the problem with 'You are awesome!' parenting is that, in hindsight, it's turned out to be completely ineffective. Research shows that merely repeating positive statements does little to raise mood or inspire achievement.[1]

And the bad news doesn't stop there. Tanith Carey, author of *Taming the Tiger Parent*, argues that exaggerating your daughter's capabilities can lead to her building a self-image based on a fantasy of superiority. Sooner or later reality will deal her a harsh blow and undermine that fantasy.[2] Empty praise affects our self-esteem in a similar way to how empty calories in sugary drinks affect our bodies: they're easy to swallow but in the long term they'll corrode you from the inside out.

Consider this: we've now had almost fifty years of 'You are awesome!' parenting and, as we showed in the Girls' Report Card in the introduction, the numbers of girls experiencing depression and anxiety are terrifying. Of course, this may be skewed by an increase in the number of distressed kids reporting their feelings of anxiousness or depression. Even if that is the case, the point remains that trying to raise kids' self-esteem with empty platitudes doesn't seem to be doing much to lessen the number of anxious and depressed kids.

This well-meaning but misguided approach to raising kids' self-esteem was based on research that showed that successful, competent people have high self-esteem. The problem is that it gets cause and effect backwards. High self-esteem doesn't breed success. It turns out that success and competence give rise to high self-esteem. The greater your ability, the more your self-esteem increases. As Martin Seligman, psychologist and author of *The Optimistic Child*, writes, 'Feelings of self-esteem in particular, and happiness in general, develop as side effects – of mastering challenges, working successfully, overcoming frustration and boredom, and winning. The feeling of self-esteem is a byproduct of doing well.'[3]

Telling little Elly that her painting of the Emma Wiggle doll was worthy of being displayed in a national gallery did not make Elly feel good, as Dad had intended. Elly may be only five, but she's not blind and she's not an idiot. She could plainly see that Jessica's painting was better than hers. Dad rushing in to solve Elly's problem by painting a picture for her did not help matters either. All that did was show Elly that, despite what Dad said, he also thinks Elly's painting is rubbish. In fact, it was so bad he needed to redo it for her.

The key to mastery

If mastery is the solution to building your daughter's self-esteem, and therefore to raising a girl who likes herself, how do you achieve it? The simple answer is, by doing.

It's not words that make our girls feel good about themselves – it is actions. And crucially, it is *their* actions. Your daughter will feel good about herself not when you tell her that she is great, but when she *does* something that *she* thinks is great. When she accomplishes a goal, learns a new skill, or does something she is proud of, she will have a sense of her own abilities. It is this feeling of mastery that will develop her self-esteem.[4] One way to instil this lesson in our girls is to live by the following rule: only do for her what she can't do for herself.

We're not talking about earth-shattering and monumental triumphs here. This rule applies to everyday activities like dressing herself, tying her own shoelaces, making her bed, carrying her schoolbag, or baking a cake where she pours in the flour and sugar and cracks the egg – and, when she's old enough, measuring out the quantities on her own. 'Children love responsibility,' says Wendy Mason, director of early learning at an independent school in Melbourne.[5] 'It's an opportunity to meet high expectations of themselves and to experience what it's like to be in the adult world.' Mason says that when children have everything done for them, they are stripped of autonomy and control in their lives. 'Is it any wonder that children in these circumstances are unable to navigate big emotions when the adults around them control all aspects of their life?'

Many times, you'll find that your daughter will not like this rule of having to do everything that she can for herself. For example, we insist our girls carry their own bags to school and preschool. It's about a 1.5 kilometre walk, so we're not talking about an overland trek. But when our girls see other children's parents carrying their schoolbags for the few metres between their car and the school gate, they tell us that we're being unfair. Our response to these complaints is a resounding, 'Whatevs.' We believe the lesson of doing what they can for themselves is more important than 'fairness'.

Of course, there are times when the chaos of life gets in the way of implementing this rule. When our girls were younger we quite often didn't have a spare thirty minutes in the morning for them to tie their own shoelaces. And wiping up morsels of spaghetti bolognese from under the dinner table and on the chairs and walls (and every other surface they'd managed to smear meat sauce on) when they were toddlers feeding themselves was not our idea of fun. But wherever possible, we try to stick by the rule because we know that every time we encourage our girls to do something for themselves, we are building their independence and mastery and demonstrating to them that we believe they can do it.

Encourage girls to speak for themselves

One important way you can help your daughter to develop her sense of mastery is to encourage her to speak for herself. This might be in social gatherings with extended family and friends or, perhaps more importantly, it could be in settings where she is meeting with authority figures, such as teachers and doctors. At the doctor's office, for example (assuming that she's old enough), encourage your daughter to give her name to the receptionist and tell the doctor what's wrong, rather than doing the talking on her behalf. We rehearse this in the car on the way to the doctor by asking our daughter to say out loud why she is going to the doctor and then asking her, 'When the doctor asks you what's wrong, what will you say?'

Therapist Liz Hogon says that one of the common factors in the kids she treats for anxiety and low self-esteem is that their parents speak for them. 'These children look over to their parent before they answer a question or watch for their parent's response when they do answer it,' says Hogon. 'If kids aren't encouraged to speak for themselves, they grow up thinking that they're not capable of having an opinion, that they are so useless they need their parent to speak for them. They also don't get to practise speaking up for themselves. They don't have self-belief.'

That lack of self-belief can affect other areas of a child's life. Primary-school principal Simon Millar has been conducting prep interviews for eleven years and in that time he's noticed a pattern. He estimates that children who are given the opportunity to speak for themselves during school interviews are around 12–18 months ahead academically compared to children whose parents answer on their behalf. It's not that the children who speak for themselves necessarily know the answers to the questions that are being asked. And it's not that the parents don't say anything at all. They may give their child little hints and encouragements to help them answer. For example, if Principal Millar asks the child what they like best at kinder and the child stares back silently, the parent might say, 'What about what you did yesterday? You brought it home and we put it on the fridge. Tell Mr Millar about that.' The child may answer with only one word – 'Painting' – and that's perfectly fine. It's not how many words that's important. What is important is that the child is given the opportunity and the responsibility to engage with someone older than themselves. The child also learns that what they have to say is important and that an adult thinks it is worth listening to.

It may be that kids who speak for themselves are ahead academically, anyhow. The fact that they have the confidence to speak up may be a result of their academic ability. But the benefits of children speaking for themselves go beyond academic performance to include the social side of schooling as well. Principal Millar says that the children who speak for themselves are also more likely to have a smoother transition into school, make friends in the classroom more easily, and show more resilience. 'While students develop at different rates to each other, it can be enhanced by parents or guardians empowering their children to speak and act for themselves, which leads to increased independence, resilience and confidence,' says Principal Millar. 'Among four-year-olds, children whose parents empower them generally show more developed academic and social skills even at such a young age.'

Don't always be there

'You're never there.'

That's how one little girl put it to her mum, sobbing because her mum wasn't going to be there to watch her sing at assembly. The assembly was in the middle of the day and the mother had a job. The previous day had featured an in-class display, also scheduled for the middle of the day. Her mother had changed her work roster to attend the in-class display, but two days in a row was a bit much. Not surprisingly, the mum left the school in tears and feeling like she'd been officially designated the Worst Mother in the World. There's nothing like that kind of guilt trip to ruin your day.

But from the point of view of developing mastery, there was an upside. This mother was teaching her daughter a valuable lesson in independence and self-reliance. While the little girl no doubt felt bad in the moment, she would also discover that doing something on her own is not the end of the world. Happy, resilient children believe they are capable of acting on their own without always having their parent as a safety net.

We are not suggesting that parents shouldn't be active participants in their child's education. Of course they should. But by not always being there, we help our children to learn internal satisfaction; achievements can be self-satisfying in their own right, they don't always need to be captured on a parent's phone to be worth doing.

But what about when the stakes are higher?

You may be thinking that the rule of letting girls do everything within their capability for themselves is fine most of the time, but what about when it's something really important? Some parents agree that tying her own shoelaces or carrying her bag is well and good, but that homework and projects are a different matter. Their reasoning springs from love and concern that their kid's education will suffer if they are not micromanaging the situation. After all, there are marks at stake that will affect their child's future progress.

But getting good marks isn't what education is about. What is equally, if not more, important is self-directed learning. This is where kids take responsibility for their own learning and pursue their own interests and passions. This is the real point of education: to become a lifelong learner, able to chart their own course and develop mastery of what matters to them, regardless of marks.

In the first three years of school we took responsibility for Violet reading her readers each night. We felt she was too young to take on that responsibility herself. But when she started bringing homework back from school, we made it clear that it was time for her to step up and take responsibility for herself. It was up to Violet to organise herself to do her homework or school projects. Or not. If she asks us for help we will gladly assist her, but we do not offer automatically. We certainly don't bribe, beg or cajole.

If Violet chooses not to do her homework, or if she forgets or does not manage her time properly, then that is her problem to deal with and she will have to face the consequences on her own. There will be no notes to teachers making excuses or asking for leniency or extensions.

You might be thinking, Aren't we worried she'll miss out on learning something? Aren't we worried she'll get into trouble? Aren't we worried that we will look like negligent parents who aren't invested in our child's education? And the answers to all these questions are: no, no and no. Empowering Violet to take responsibility for her actions – rather than continuing to rely on us – is more important than any content on a take-home worksheet. The other benefit of this approach is there is no yelling and fighting over homework in our house. If Violet says she doesn't want to do homework, we say, 'Okay, that's your decision. You can explain it to your teacher.'

Since we know that there is little to no academic benefit from homework in primary school (as we discussed in the chapter about calm), the only good that can come from it is the opportunity for Violet to develop independence. If we intervened unnecessarily and started taking responsibility for Violet completing her homework and projects, we would be undermining quite possibly the only benefit of homework.

If parents micromanage or even complete their child's homework or project, they risk implicitly sending their child a message: you can't do this on your own. Even though it is motivated by love and concern for their child's education, too much parental intervention may corrode their child's confidence in their own abilities and their opportunity to develop mastery.

To be clear, we are not suggesting that you should never help your daughter with her projects or homework. But the key word here is 'help'. For example, when Violet was doing her maths homework and she ran out of fingers to count on, we reached for a bag of frozen peas and showed her how to use them instead. And we've spent many weekends driving around procuring cardboard boxes, paint, masking tape and God knows what else that our girls said they needed for their projects. We've also advised on issues such as time management. For instance, when Violet wanted to make her water-cycle landscape project out of papier-mâché, we explained that it was going to take days to dry in between each step and suggested that she start early. But we still left it up to Violet to decide what she was going to do and when she was going to do it. If she didn't get organised in time to do her papier-mâché then she would experience the natural consequences of that decision.

Sometimes it's really hard not to intervene. For example, when Violet was in grade one she was given a project that required cutting and pasting text and images into a homemade book. And let us tell you, at the age of six Violet had the cutting and pasting skills of, well, a six-year-old. She spent hours on this book full of jagged edges, uneven borders and odd angles. It was excruciating to watch, knowing that we could have cut and pasted the text for her in about ten minutes and it would have looked a hell of a lot neater. But what would that have taught Violet? That she's so bad at cutting and pasting that we need to do it for her. That our judgement about the quality of her work is more important than her own. And that she doesn't need to take responsibility for her own learning because we will swoop in and do it for her.

Kids are clueless – and that is their superpower

Children, particularly young children, are clueless. And that is a good thing. In fact, it's their superpower. They have no clue about their abilities, or where the limits of those abilities might lie. Consequently, they will attempt new tasks and challenges no matter what. As educational commentator and author Sir Kenneth Robinson explained in one of the most watched TED Talks in history, 'Kids will take a chance. If they don't know, they'll have a go. They're not frightened of being wrong.'[6]

Robinson illustrated his point with the story of a six-year-old girl who rarely paid attention in class until one day her teacher asked the children to draw a picture. The little girl became thoroughly absorbed in the task of drawing. Fascinated, her teacher went over to the girl and asked what she was drawing. The girl replied, 'I'm drawing a picture of God.' The teacher said, 'But nobody knows what God looks like.' And the girl said, 'They will in a minute.'

Robinson argued that as we grow up, we lose this ability to have a go. Watch a baby try to walk and you'll see that making mistakes is how children naturally learn and develop. Because they have not yet learned to fear failure, and they have no concept of making a mistake, children try and try again – and keep trying. They pursue independence and mastery with endless determination and single-minded focus.

But for many girls, somewhere between conquering walking and becoming an adult, the fear of failure becomes a stronger motivator than the desire for mastery and independence. Many girls come to think that making mistakes is the worst thing they can possibly do. They learn to fear failure from watching and modelling themselves after us, from the way our education system expects kids to colour within the lines, and from the all-pervasive pressure on girls to be perfect. When children become afraid of failure they limit their potential, they make their world small, they can suffer anxiety and crippling fears, they refuse to step out of their comfort zones, and they lose the ability and drive to achieve mastery.

Celebrating failure

When you step back and allow your daughter to do things for herself, she will fail. She is going to screw up, make messes and mismanage situations because she is still learning and figuring out how the world works. You can count on it.

So the question is, should you allow your daughter to fail?

The answer is yes. Allow her to fail. Allow her to feel that what she is doing isn't measuring up to her own standards.

Then allow her to fail again. And then again. And then some more.

Mastery is something that can only be developed the hard way – through frustration, persistence, failing and trying again. Some kids who have extraordinary talent or luck may be able to take a shortcut on this path but, in general, there is only one way to mastery and it is paved with discomfort. When we don't allow our girls to fail we are depriving them of the opportunity to achieve mastery, and with it real and enduring self-esteem. This is the kind of self-esteem that is necessary for a girl to like herself.

When Violet was a toddler and we hadn't yet thought through the importance of allowing children to fail, we were your typical over-protective, over-anxious, over-attentive first-time parents. We would routinely lift Violet up onto climbing equipment at the park that we thought she was not yet strong or coordinated enough to manage on her own. We took responsibility for navigating her physical play. Her expectation that we would help her became so ingrained that she would stand at the bottom of the equipment, raise her arms and look to us. She didn't even attempt to climb onto the equipment herself. Without intending to, we had taught Violet that she was not capable. It was astounding just how quickly we had instilled helplessness in her.

By the time Ivy came along, two things had changed. Firstly, we were more relaxed and had less time to helicopter over our girls. But we'd also realised the importance of failure. We rarely helped Ivy navigate playground equipment. When she would chuck a tantrum because she couldn't mount the climbing frame, we empathised with her frustration but then we would explain to her that she needed to keep practising and trying different ways to climb the equipment and then, in time, she would be able to do it. It got to the point where it didn't even occur to Ivy that we could help her. She took 100 per cent responsibility for achieving her own playground goals. And when she did, the look of satisfaction and pride on her face was wonderful. Reflecting back, every time we lifted Violet onto a climbing frame to spare her the frustration, we denied her the opportunity to experience the same pride and satisfaction that Ivy had.

We know: this sounds like a parenting handbook written by the US Marine Corps. But this needn't be a brutal lesson that the world is an icy-cold place and life is just one bitter defeat after another. As with most situations, it all depends on context and how you present it to your daughter. You may have to work to reframe failure as desirable. Here's one example of how to teach girls to embrace failure.

Chris's story

During a parent-helper reading lesson at Violet's school, I was working with a little girl who had already learned to fear failure. She read each word tentatively, constantly looking to me for feedback and reassurance. When she came to a word that was unfamiliar, she'd just stop and look at me with big round eyes, waiting for me to jump in and help her. She was so concerned about making mistakes that she wouldn't even attempt to sound out the word without me starting her off. Silence was better than showing the world that she did not know something.

I felt like the lesson was going to take an eternity, so I told her my one rule about reading.

'You have to make mistakes.' In fact, I told her, 'I want to hear you make as many mistakes as possible.'

She looked up at me, confused and a little suspicious. When the whole point of school is about learning to get things right, being told to make mistakes just seemed like a trick.

'Do you know why you should be making mistakes?' I asked. She shook her head. 'Because that's how we know we're learning.'

The lesson continued, and every time the little girl tried and made a mistake, I praised her loudly for her courage. Every mistake was a celebration. It was the triumph of getting in and having a go. Only after she'd tried and tried again did we sound out the word together. And it turned out that she knew many more words than she thought she did. She just needed to try them out.

Of course, this doesn't apply just to reading. It applies to every major life skill, from maths to learning how to blow a bubble with bubblegum. A mantra for life: if you're not making mistakes, you're not learning.

The curse of perfection

Another reason to encourage your daughter to embrace her mistakes is that it will help protect her against perfectionism. Girls and women are frequently conditioned not to show the world anything but their best. 'I'm a perfectionist' is often used as a humble brag. But scratch beneath the shiny surface of perfectionism and you will see a festering pit of insecurity and anxiety. No one can be perfect all the time – even a self-proclaimed perfectionist knows this about themselves. So naturally any person who has built their identity on being perfect will live in a constant state of fear of letting the cracks show in their facade. It is very difficult for a perfectionist to truly like themselves because deep down they will feel like a fraud, knowing they are one mistake away from being exposed.

Like all people, your daughter is going to make mistakes in her life, and lots of them. If she is going to like herself then she needs to know that failure is not a measure of her character or her worth. When parents encourage their daughter to make mistakes, failure becomes less scary. She will know that she has permission to try new things, fail or stuff up royally, and then try again. She will also learn through her own experience that the world will not disintegrate if she is not perfect.

Failing is not the same as being a failure

Given society's obsession with success, celebrating failure seems counterintuitive, if not outright perverse. All of us want to see our daughters succeed, so we need to make an important distinction between being a failure and failing well. To *be* a failure is an all-encompassing identity. If girls internalise the idea that they are a failure in their inner core, it's likely they'll lower their expectations for themselves and the expectations for the world around them. After all, what's the point of trying if the outcome is (in their minds at least) predetermined? It's important to understand that failure is not a character trait but a necessary step on the path to mastery.

Failing well, in contrast, is falling, getting back up, and learning from the experience. It's about helping our girls to realise that failure doesn't define them. Rather, failure is the cost of entry to trying new things. Teaching your daughter to fail well doesn't mean that she is going to grow up to be a failure. Quite the contrary, failing means she had the courage to try something. It didn't work out, so now she can learn from it and then do better next time (or perhaps the time after that).

People often talk about learning from mistakes but they neglect to mention that it is a skill in itself. Many adults never really learn how to learn. They try something, don't get the results that they wanted or expected, and then go and repeat the exact same process. Eventually, many get frustrated and give up.

The skill of learning how to learn from failure is something that parents can help their daughter develop. It requires a process of reflection about what went well and what didn't go so well and noticing a pattern, so that your daughter can refine her approach as needed. You can aid that process by encouraging your daughter to try again, but to try in a different way. Ask her what she did that time and what the result was. Prompt her to think about what she could do differently next time to get a different result.

If you don't like the word 'failure', then substitute it for another F-word: 'feedback'. Failure is feedback that what you tried didn't work, or didn't work as you expected it would. You can use that feedback to refine your approach and have another go. Feedback is only useful when it actually does *feed* back into whatever we're doing and spark us to rethink and re-evaluate.

Allow her to own her success

The flipside of embracing failure is embracing success. When your daughter succeeds at something she found difficult, make a big deal of it. Turn it into a story that shows that courage and failure are a necessary part of success. For example: 'At first getting to the top of the climbing frame was really hard. You fell off quite a few times. That felt frustrating, didn't it? But you didn't give up. You tried something different and worked out that if you climb up the pole first you can step onto the frame. Now the climbing frame is easy for you. Yay for you!'

Allow her to own her success. This may be quite different from how you were raised. When we were growing up, for example, kids were often taught to be falsely modest – especially girls. Girls who owned their success were accused of having 'tickets on themselves', being 'full of themselves', having 'a big head' or 'showing off'.

To avoid these labels, you might have grown up making comments like, 'That was so unexpected,' or, 'I just got lucky,' even when you'd spent weeks working your guts out. Or you may have said, 'I didn't really deserve it,' because to take credit for your hard work, persistence and talents would have seemed vulgar and conceited.

The problem is that every time a girl utters these self-deprecating comments, a small part of her believes it. Diminishing her success in order to fit in with the expectations of others is a way of diminishing herself. The more she repeats these statements, the more likely she is to take them as fact rather than the false statements of modesty they really are. What's worse, she's also corroding her power perspective by surrendering to external forces for her success, even if that external force is dumb luck.

Just as we should encourage our daughter to own her failures, we should encourage her to own her successes. Of course, she should recognise the help and support other people give her – nobody is a self-made woman (or man, for that matter) – but don't let her look for external reasons to credit her success to. Sure, some people get where they are through some good luck and the right circumstances, but in most cases there's a much bigger dollop of courage, hard work, skill, determination and acceptance of failure that ensures continued success.

We don't tolerate false modesty in our daughters. When our girls succeed, we celebrate their achievement. We tell them they should feel proud of themselves. We model this ourselves, telling them, 'I'm proud I did that myself,' or, 'I worked really hard at that and I did a great job.' When someone gives us a compliment, we accept it and say thank you, rather than building an ironclad case as to why we don't deserve it.

The myth of comparison and competition

We live in a competitive culture and our learning and mastery are often judged by who we outshine. The notion that competition brings out the best in people is taken as fact. If we didn't have competition, so the theory goes, we'd all settle for dull mediocrity. According to this idea, competition makes us strive for excellence. It builds character. And if we're still unconvinced, we tell ourselves that competition is just a part of life. It's a dog-eat-dog world out there, so our girls might as well get used to it. The sooner girls learn to deal with competition, the better.

The logic of competition seems pretty compelling – at first. But if you look more closely, the cracks begin to appear. Research shows that competition does not make our children perform better. In fact, the stress of competition actually undermines their performance. For example, children who were told that they were competing in computer games performed more poorly than those who were not told they were competing.[7] Children who are constantly competing and comparing themselves with others can have brittle confidence because they see the world as a brutal, unwelcoming, winner-takes-all place.[8] If their self-worth is built on being the best, then when they inevitably lose, they are left with a crushing sense of themselves as a failure.

Over half a century of research shows that children learn better when they work collaboratively. They display superior problem-solving skills, they are more creative and, crucially, they have better self-esteem.[9] US education expert Alfie Kohn, who has been studying the effects of competition for three decades, says our kids are losing as a result of our push to make them winners. 'Most people lose in most competitive encounters, and it's obvious why that causes self-doubt,' writes Kohn in his book *No Contest: The case against competition.* 'But even winning doesn't build character; it just lets a child gloat temporarily . . . Your value is defined by what you've done. Worse – you're a good person in proportion to the number of people you've beaten.'[10]

Being constantly judged, compared and pressured – not just at preschool and school, but in dance class, at a gymnastics meet, or on the soccer field – can chip away at a girl's wellbeing. Competition is an external measure that positions a girl's performance and associated self-worth as relative to other people's. There is little place for intrinsic motivation in a competitive mindset. It relies on girls doing an activity to be measured, evaluated and rated, rather than doing it because it is inherently satisfying and brings them joy.

Our aim should be to raise girls who like themselves *all the time* – not only when they are beating someone else. Whenever possible we need to push back against this culture of competitiveness by encouraging our daughters to find worth in the activities they do on their own, rather than endlessly comparing themselves to others. If your daughter complains, 'Why aren't I as good as [insert friend's name]?' challenge her to ask herself why it matters if someone else is better than she is. How does that affect her enjoyment or achievement? Ask her why she's engaged in the activity in the first place. Is it because it's fun and because she wants to learn? Or is it because she wants to win or be the best?

If your daughter only does something in order to be better than others, then it's more than likely she'll end up a loser. To be more precise, she'll end up with the perspective that she is a loser because no matter how good your daughter is, there is someone, somewhere, who will be better than she is. Comparing herself to others might work in the short term, but in the long term it's a recipe for feeling inadequate.

It's for this reason that we need to be careful about making comparisons when praising our daughters. It's common for parents to try to make their daughter feel good by telling her she was the best dancer on the stage or that she's the smartest or best-behaved kid in her class. While these parents are no doubt motivated by love and think they're building self-esteem, pointing out that their daughter is superior to her peers can have the opposite effect. It can create anxiety and insecurity in the girl because the natural assumption is that when she is not the best, she is not good enough. The other risk of telling your daughter that she's better than other kids is that she is likely to repeat it and end up upsetting her friends.

We try to avoid comparative praise at all times. When our girls do well at their gymnastics display, or taekwondo grading, or on a spelling test, we praise them for practising, stretching themselves outside their comfort zones and trying their best. It's about them, not their performance relative to everyone else. This doesn't mean that we thwart our girls' ambitions. Nor does it mean we're raising self-absorbed narcissists whose only concern is their own limited experience. We want our girls to be driven to succeed and a big part of this is not relying on other people's perceived inferiority in order to feel okay about themselves. Instead of talking to our girls about where they came in the race or test relative to their peers, we ask them if they were happy with how they performed. Do they think they made the right choices? Do they think they should act differently next time?

We also celebrate the achievements of other children, so our girls learn that other people's success does not detract from their own success and self-worth. When another child wins an award or prize, even if it's something Violet or Ivy really wanted for themselves, we encourage them to congratulate that other child and to flex their empathy muscles by trying to feel happy for them.

Using praise to foster mastery

Other ways to use praise to encourage your daughter's independence and mastery, rather than undermine it, include:

1. *Keeping it real*
Make sure that your praise is honest. This is the opposite of the empty or blanket praise dished out with 'You are awesome!' parenting. Children, just like adults, pick up on hollow flattery. They know when we're putting it on. Praise your daughter

for something that she has actually done or is capable of doing herself. It's unlikely that any child will fail utterly and completely. It's more likely that, in any situation, there are elements of their performance or outcome that merit praise.

2. *Praising persistence and tasks she can replicate*
Reserve praise for the tasks your daughter can control and do again in the future. This is more likely to make her feel empowered and motivated. For example, praise her for her hard work and commitment in completing her project (something she can control and replicate) rather than her good mark (something that the teacher ultimately controls and your daughter may not be able to influence next time).

Too often we focus on the final masterpiece, and forget the hours of effort that went into making it. Rather than praising her painting, tell her, 'I really like how you tried a different technique this time. Practising is how you will become a better painter.' Research shows that praising the work process ('You're using good puzzle-solving strategies!') rather than children's talent ('You must be really good at puzzles!') enhances their self-motivation.[11]

Praising your daughter for practising and trying, even when she didn't get the results she wanted, is far more valuable than celebrating the end result. It sends a message to your daughter about what's really important. It shows that you value skills – persistence and practice – that she can apply to many other areas of her life beyond what she's being praised for. Persistence is a skill that will serve her well throughout her lifetime, no matter what she puts her mind to.

Reframe other people's successes and achievements in terms of their work ethic rather than natural gifts. When we talk about our daughters' uncle who is a highly accomplished and awarded composer, we will say, 'Your uncle Michael plays the piano so well because he practises every day.' This has the added benefit of showing our daughters that what might seem completely out of their reach now may actually be achievable – as long as they put in the practice. After all, if they believe that music is something only musically gifted people can do, then they'll never bother trying. This also applies to everyday activities. When Violet told us that her friend Jeremy is better at Minecraft than her, we reminded her, 'That's because Jeremy has practised a lot more than you have. If you practise more you'll get better too.'

3. *Measuring progress backwards*
The road to mastery is often long and arduous. If your daughter becomes discouraged, praise her for how far she has come from her starting point. For example, 'When you started school the only word you could read was your name. Now you are reading chapter books. That's because you practise your reading every night. Yay for you!' Rather than focusing on how far away she is from her goal, and potentially making her feel daunted by the long road ahead, remind her of how far she has progressed to motivate her to keep going.

4. *Praising your daughter for doing activities that she finds difficult*
Your daughter is more likely to persist with behaviours and activities she struggles with if you acknowledge the difficulty and praise her for trying. We're not talking about playing a Bach piano concerto or memorising characters in Mandarin. It could be everyday activities such as waiting, sharing or practising skills that don't come easily to her. For example, 'I can see that was really tricky for you. But you kept going. Well done.'

Brace yourself for rejection

Raising independent, masterful children is bittersweet. If you do it properly, you'll eventually make yourself redundant as a parent. Or your role as a parent will shrink to the point where you might as well be redundant. It happens by stages.

For example, after the first term of prep we stopped walking Violet into class. She had a few objections to this new plan. She pointed out the other parents who were walking their children to class. But we knew that this was a completely safe situation for Violet and her objections were based on her perception that she couldn't do it. We wanted her to know that she was capable of doing it by herself. The best we could do for our daughter was to help her understand that she was brave enough and competent enough to do this on her own. When we picked her up from school, we praised her for being so mature and brave.

Of course, she didn't immediately listen to our little pep talk. And our praise about being brave didn't seem to make a dent. The next day, sure enough, was groundhog day. She again wanted us to walk her into class, but we told her she could do it on her own. This went on for a couple more days.

Then one day, she not only didn't ask us to walk her into class, she also took the hand of another girl who was crying and walked her into class. If all our thoughts popped up above our heads like a social media stream, you would have seen #SmugParenting Moment hovering there. Our little girl had acted independently and felt strong enough to help another child learn the lesson that she had. #AirPunch

But as we found out a year later, pushing our girls to be independent is not without pain. One day we were running late for school and it was raining. Violet's class had already gone inside so we went to walk her into class. When we got to the top of the stairs, Violet stopped and said, 'It's okay, you can stay here.'

Time to fight back the tears. We were thrilled at her independence. Isn't this what we wanted for her? Isn't this what we worked to create? But our little girl, our six-year-old, had rejected us. Wasn't this about five years ahead of schedule? We weren't prepared for it.

That's what parenting is about: we are raising our children to not need us. If we do our job well our kids will reject us, not because they don't want us or like us, but because they are independent and masterful. Raising children is like flying a kite; bit by bit we release the string to let them fly higher. Sometimes we need to reel the string back in a bit. The trick is to work out why you're reeling it back. Is it for your own comfort, or is it from concern that she is venturing further into heavy winds that will surely crush her? Only you can be the judge. You won't always get it right. Then again, no one does. We all make the best call we can in any situation with the available information. But our job as parents, day by day and year by year, is to loosen our grip on our girls and let them soar.

Action for dads

When you stuff up, let your daughter see it.

You may have worked this out already: you are your daughter's hero. This makes you the perfect person to teach her that mistakes are not something to fear but are just part of the processes of learning and mastery. Let's face it: if *you* can screw up from time to time, then anyone can.

Help your daughter embrace failure by telling her about the skills that you're still working on and developing but have yet to master – and what you're planning to do better. This could be anything from baking to your tennis backhand. Tell her about times you made a right mess of something. Give her the most excruciatingly embarrassing examples that you can think of in all their age-appropriate gory detail. The lesson is that even though you made a mess, the world didn't end and that, while you may have regrets, you still lived to tell the tale and try again. Show her with your own experiences that not only is it *okay* to make mistakes, it's natural, normal and unavoidable. Remind her that she should never, ever let the fear of failure stand in her way.

Recap

- You cannot give your daughter self-esteem by showering her with word presents. Her self-esteem needs to grow from within. It is *her* actions that will make her feel independent and masterful, not your words.
- The road to mastery is paved with frustration, mistakes and discomfort. Rather than trying to protect your daughter from failure, help her to learn to fail well.
- Praise has the potential to empower your daughter or cripple her. To develop your daughter's mastery and independence, make sure your praise is honest. She'll know when you're lying. Praise her effort, her persistence and her courage to do things that she finds hard.
- Our bittersweet job as parents is to eventually make ourselves redundant.
- To raise an independent, masterful girl who likes herself, only do for her what she cannot do for herself.

6

A girl who likes herself has strong relationships

Ten years ago Canadian primary-school teacher Dana Kerford started to notice something odd about her students. On some days, the kids in her maths class were curious little sponges, soaking up the contents of her lessons. On other days, they were sieves, barely able to retain anything from the lessons. Kerford started looking for a pattern to explain the difference in her students' willingness and ability to learn. She quickly discovered that one of the most significant factors influencing whether or not her class learned anything that day had nothing to do with her lesson plan or her abilities as a teacher. What *did* seem to make a difference was what had happened in the schoolyard at playtime. When her students felt like they didn't have any friends, were being excluded from a friendship group, or were struggling to deal with conflict, teasing or bullying, they became so preoccupied with and overwhelmed by what was going on in their social lives that they were unable to learn. Kerford realised that if she wanted her class to master fractions or geometry, she first had to teach them how to get along with each other. This insight led her on a journey to teach children social skills in order to strengthen their relationships with their peers, deal with conflict in productive ways and reduce their friendship problems.

Kerford has since learned she's not alone in noticing the link between academic learning and social skills. 'When I am at an education conference I ask teachers to raise their hand if they have seen that a student's learning or their wellbeing has been negatively impacted by an issue with a friend. Every teacher raises their hand,' she says. Education departments, schools and parents spend oodles of money, time and effort developing, measuring and endlessly critiquing the best methods to teach our children to read, write and add numbers. But one of the biggest advantages we can give our daughters to boost their learning is to teach them how to be a good friend.

The benefits of strong social skills go beyond the classroom. Kids who have secure friendships based on trust and mutual respect are more comfortable and less anxious in new situations; they are able to be assertive, stating their wishes clearly, and are less likely to be swayed by others.[1] Children who develop good social skills grow up to be more successful adults,[2] and positive relationships are the top protective factor against depression, anxiety, other mental health disorders and loneliness.[3] Loneliness, in particular, is being called the social equivalent of cancer – and is every bit as deadly.[4]

In this chapter we are going to detail techniques you might like to use to help your daughter enhance her friendships and social skills, so she is able to create more meaningful connections with people. As you'll see, strong peer friendships are just one kind of relationship a girl who likes herself has. This chapter will also cover the importance of building a good 'support crew' around your daughter to nurture, inspire and guide her and keep her safe. We've also included a couple of bang-for-buck strategies that can help strengthen your own relationship with your daughter.

Do we really need to teach our kids social skills?

One reason we don't teach social skills is that people tend to assume they develop naturally. It's almost as if kids just 'get' the social skills update in the same way that you get an auto-update on your phone's software. But the idea that kids, and the adults they become, automatically acquire social skills is a myth.

Sceptical? Just take a look around at your colleagues, or perhaps your extended family at Christmas, and it's pretty obvious that not everyone learned these skills organically in the playground. Some people are able to effortlessly put others at ease and connect, while other people seem to career from one friendship dumpster fire to another. Most of us fall somewhere in between these extremes. We're pretty good with some people and in some contexts, while in others we just can't seem to connect.

As child and family mental health expert Claire Orange says:

Social skills are just like any other skill. We wouldn't give a child a book and expect them to know which was the front and which was the back, and how to decode the words. We start slowly and stack the skills on top of each other. And yet when it comes to social skills we expect that we can plonk a child out there in the middle of other children and they'll get it. It's the rare child who doesn't need social skill building, just like any other skill.

Maybe your daughter will be one of those lucky people who develops excellent social skills on her own. But why risk it? Why not help her learn the tools required to develop and maintain strong relationships, now and throughout her whole life?

The eyes have it

When it comes to building your daughter's social skills, a good place to start is the eyes. Specifically, eye contact. Developing and maintaining eye contact is fundamental to how we relate to each other. As every magazine editor and marketing expert knows, images that show a model's eyes sell better. Our brains are so primed to see faces that we'll find them even when they're not there. Clouds, soccer balls and the moon are just some of the unlikely objects people have claimed to have seen faces in.

Some children learn to make eye contact by modelling the adults around them, but others may require it to be spelled out for them. Your daughter may need to be explicitly told that she should make eye contact when she meets people and when she is speaking to someone. You can help by regularly reminding her to look at people who say hello to her and to maintain eye contact during a conversation. Ordering in cafes and restaurants, and speaking to people in shops or in a doctor's office are all perfect ways for her to develop this habit. If you're in a cafe, prompt your daughter to look at the serving staff when she orders, and again when she says thank you when her food arrives. Remind her to look at the doctor when she answers or asks a question.

As with teaching most skills to children, she will probably need roughly nine hundred gazillion reminders before it becomes habit.

Although getting your daughter to make eye contact may be easier said than done, especially if she is naturally shy, don't let this one slide. As harsh as it may sound, in a few years' time the world is not going to care if your daughter is shy or not. If she does not make eye contact she will be seen as rude, cold or unfriendly, which will make it harder for her to find friends, have influence, be listened to and even get a job.

And at the risk of going all *How to Win Friends and Influence People*, there are some other basic skills that you may have to explicitly teach your daughter, which will be a big help in making and maintaining friendships: smiling, having a friendly yet confident voice, and using people's names.[5] In the car on the way to birthday parties and other social occasions, we ask our girls if they can remember the names of their friends' parents and other family members. We get them to repeat each name to help them remember it and then prompt them to use those names when they say hello, goodbye and thank you for inviting them. Similarly, on the way to the doctor we remind our girls of the doctor's name and encourage them to use it.

The art of conversation

Think back to that dinner party where you had the misfortune of sitting next to the person who had the social skills of a turnip. A whole night went by and they didn't ask a single question about you, or anyone or anything else for that matter. You probably went home exhausted from the emotional labour of having to fill the awkward silences all night. Chances are you have no desire to see that person again, let alone establish a friendship with them. It could be that that person was just a particularly self-absorbed turnip. More generously, it's possible that they never learned the rules of conversation.

Conversation is a form of play. And just like any other kind of play, conversation works best when the participants share and take turns. One person asks someone a question and then listens to their answer. Then it's the other person's turn to ask a question while you listen to their answer. Education expert Dr Allen Mendler recommends teaching kids how to take turns in conversations by using a talking stick. The child who holds the stick talks, while the other child(ren) listen. When the stick-holder has asked a question, they then pass the stick to the other child to answer. After the new stick-holder answers the question, they get to ask a question before passing the stick to the responder.[6] Alternatively, you could give the same physical conversation prompts by playing a game of catch or passing a doll back and forth. When your daughter has the ball/doll she speaks; when she doesn't she listens.

The important point, though, is that sometimes children (and some adults) will use their turn to speak to only talk about themselves. It doesn't occur to them to ask questions. They might also not be great at listening. Waiting for a gap in the discussion so you can resume talking about yourself is one way to kill a conversation.

When it comes to social interaction, asking questions is a superpower. A single question has the power to break the ice, fill an awkward silence and convey to someone that you think they are interesting and important.

Asking questions is a skill that will help your girls in the playground and the boardroom and every social arena in between. We encourage our girls to ask people questions by modelling it, and also explaining to them that asking someone a question is kind. Asking a question is a way of telling someone that they matter.

Let her speak

We need to add a caveat to our advice about teaching your daughter to be a good questioner and listener. We are not advocating that you raise a lovely compliant listener who does not feel empowered or have the skills to express her own opinions or talk about herself. Socially, many women often play the role of audience member, listening and politely exclaiming at regular intervals during other people's monologues. The last thing we want is to contribute to the socialisation of a new generation of people-pleasers who are very good at putting others at ease at the expense of their own need for self-expression and connection. To balance our question-asking lessons, we regularly encourage our daughters to express their own ideas and opinions to us and other people. For example, if the conversation drifts to a movie, book or place our girls are familiar with, we will say, 'Violet's seen that movie. Violet, tell us what you thought about it,' or, 'We went there on holidays. Ivy, how about you tell them what you liked best about it.'

Being friends is not the same as being the same

Making eye contact and asking questions are the foundations of social interaction. But developing and maintaining friendships requires more, of course. Frequently, finding a common interest is a starting place for a girl to make a new friend. A typical friendship-starting conversation among children might go something like this:

Girl 1: 'Do you play basketball?'

Girl 2: 'Yeah, I play basketball.'

Girl 1: 'I play for x team. What team are you on?'

While finding a common interest is a great place to start when making friends, girls often think that they must share *everything* in order to remain friends. Where boys seem to be fine moving between interests, girls often appear to believe that in order to be friends with someone they have to like the same activities, have the same taste in fashion, have the same hairstyle, and so on. You may have to explicitly tell your daughter that she and her playmates can still be friends even if their interests do not coincide. On. Absolutely. Everything.

In practice this may be:

- It's okay if your friend doesn't want three pigtails (the third being a unicorn horn, obviously). You can still be friends.
- It's okay if you like playing with Sarah and your friend doesn't. Not everybody gets along with everyone. You can play with Sarah sometimes and with your other friend other times.
- It's okay that you think dogs are better than cats and your friend thinks the opposite. You don't have to agree on everything to be friends.

Similarly, girls can make the mistake of thinking that once they have made a friend, they should do everything together all the time. They might worry that if they do not play with their friend every playtime or sit next to them every snack time then the friendship will be over.

In her friendship workshops, Dana Kerford teaches children that sometimes different friends are good in different situations. For example, one friend might be great to work with in class but they might not be the best person to play with at lunchtime because your daughter likes to play on the monkey bars and her friend would rather go to the library. At lunchtime your daughter might have a different friend she prefers to play with on the monkey bars and yet this girl might not be a good person to work with in class because she is too distracting. You might need to explain to your daughter that that's okay; she can still be friends with both children without being disloyal to either of them.

You may also need to explicitly state to your daughter that friends don't always have to play together. Sometimes your daughter might like to play by herself or play a different game – and that's okay. You can help her navigate this tricky situation by practising what to say. It might be, 'I want to play by myself now,' or, 'I'm painting right now – I'll play with you later.' Giving her the framework for what to say to her friends can be useful, helping her to smooth over what she might find a stressful or difficult social situation. Similarly, you might need to help your daughter understand that if her friend doesn't want to play with her one playtime then it is not the end of the friendship – or the end of the world.

Friendship is a choice

One piece of advice we've given our daughters in the past is that they should be friends with everyone. But now we're not so sure this is such good advice. Our 'Be friends with everyone' theory came from a good place. We didn't want our girls to be deliberately cruel or hurtful to other people. But if we're really honest, we were treating friendships like a numbers game: the more the better.

Kerford says that encouraging children to be friends with everybody is a bad idea. 'If parents are telling kids to be friends with everyone they are giving dangerous advice because not everyone is good for us,' she says. 'Some people bring out the best in us and some people bring out the worst, and children should not have to be friends with people who are not good for them.'

Kerford assures parents that they don't need to worry if their child doesn't have a big group of friends. 'One good friend is much better than a whole group of unhealthy friendships,' she says.

The desire to be friends with everyone can lead children into situations where they try to 'fit in' rather than find 'belonging'. The two are not the same. As social scientist and author Brené Brown writes in *The Gifts of Imperfection*, 'Fitting in is about assessing a situation and becoming who you need to be to be accepted. Belonging, on the other hand, doesn't require us to change who we are; it requires us to be who we are.'[7]

Fitting in is changing yourself to conform more closely to some external idea of who you should be. But as counterintuitive as it might sound, in order to 'belong' you have to be prepared *not* to 'fit in'.

'[M]en and women who have the deepest sense of true belonging are people who also have the courage to stand alone when called to do that. They are willing to maintain their integrity and risk disconnection in order to stand up for what they believe in,' Brown says.

To put that in kid-speak: only give your friendship to someone who likes you the way you are and who you like the way they are.

If you're not convinced, think about how trying to be friends with everyone might play out later in life. 'What does that advice mean in romantic relationships?' asks Kerford. 'That's not when we want our kids learning the importance of being selective for the very first time. The message we want to give our kids is choose wisely. What's so special about friendship is that it's a relationship that we choose.'

This isn't to say that we should raise our girls to be antisocial and deliberately exclusionary. We can still encourage our daughters to be kind and respectful to others without telling them they must be friends with them all. We should simply apply the same rules to childhood friendships that we apply to adult relationships. As adults, we don't expect to be friends with everyone. While we endeavour to be polite and respectful to all our acquaintances and colleagues – well, most of us, most of the time anyway – we don't feel compelled to share our secrets with every single one of them or invite them all to our birthday party. Rather than focusing on the quantity of friends, we should be teaching our kids about the importance of quality friends.

What makes a good friend?

Sometimes it is difficult for children to spot the difference between a healthy friendship and a toxic one. Hell, sometimes it's hard for adults too. In the absence of other information, kids do what most of us do: in situations where they are uncertain, they'll watch the behaviour of others to deduce what to do. Often that means saying and doing what others are doing. Applied to friendships, this might mean assuming that popular kids are good friends. After all, there must be a reason that the popular kids are the popular kids.

Of course, it doesn't always work like that. The popular kids might be great. But girls can sometimes find that they can't truly be themselves among the popular kids. Or they may discover that they are not welcome anyway. Audrey Monke is a psychologist and social skills expert, and she argues that trying to fit in with the popular kids can lead to lopsided and unfulfilling friendships, where often only the child who's trying to fit in values the friendship.

'Rather than encouraging children to continue forcing themselves into a friendship or a group where they are not wholeheartedly welcome, help them instead discover where their real "tribe" is. This "tribe" might not be huge. In fact, it may be with just one or two other like-minded kids,' says Monke.[8]

This can be a really tough message for children to understand when popularity seems to be everything. The following kid-friendly checklist provides a good starting place to have these conversations with your daughter.

A good friend:

- is fun to be with
- makes me feel happy and good about myself most of the time
- is kind to me
- respects me
- is trustworthy
- keeps my secrets
- takes turns and is fair
- listens to what I say and cares about my feelings
- stands up for me
- likes me just the way I am.

This list is a great way for girls to recognise who in their peer group is their true friend. We have also found it useful in helping our daughters realise when someone is not a good friend for them.

Recognising the need for quality friends will become increasingly important as our girls get older and enter the world of social media. If they are not careful they could spend a huge amount of time and energy accruing thousands of 'followers' and 'friends' and still not have a single person outside their family in their life they can trust and who genuinely values them for who they are.

I'm not your friend anymore!

If you've been around a group of children for any length of time, chances are you've heard, 'I'm not your friend anymore!' A child who says something like this has not yet learned that real friendship is more robust than one disagreement or conflict. If your friendships dissolved after one mistake or disagreement, how many friends would you have left? That's why it's a good idea to tell your daughter that she doesn't have to get along with her friends all of the time. Sometimes they will make her upset, sometimes she will make them upset. And that's okay. What matters is what happens *after* she or her friend becomes upset. Helping your daughter to negotiate bumps in the road of friendships is an important skill that will serve her throughout her life.

We both grew up in households where unless the other child had broken one of our bones or made us bleed, we were told to ignore their bad behaviour. But reflecting back, this response has the effect of disempowering children. It tells them that other people can treat them badly and they should just put up with it.

Rather than telling your daughter to just walk away from or ignore someone who's treating her badly, it's more effective to teach her the skills to deal with poor behaviour in a productive way. Kerford's name for this is the 'quick comeback'. The basic idea is that when someone intentionally does something or says something that's mean, your daughter needs to be able to respond instantly in an assertive and clear yet polite manner.

Examples of quick comebacks include:

- That's not okay.
- That was really mean.
- I don't like that.
- Excuse me!
- Knock it off.

Delivery is everything. To be effective, your daughter's quick comeback must be said with authority. For extra impact, Signe Whitson, a child and adolescent emotional and behavioural health expert and author of *8 Keys to End Bullying*, recommends using the person's name so your daughter can convey that she is unafraid and on an equal footing.[9] What's important in a quick comeback is that it is assertive, non-blaming and non-inflammatory. You don't want your daughter to respond to poor behaviour with equally poor behaviour. To borrow the famous words of Michelle Obama, when the other child goes low, your daughter can use her quick comeback to go high. After she has delivered it, your daughter should walk away so that the conflict does not escalate.

Most of us think of our best comebacks ten minutes too late, or the next day in the shower. Your daughter will be no different. So the key to a quick comeback is rehearsal. Practise with your daughter – the statement and the delivery – so in the heat of the moment she will be ready. We have role-played quick comebacks with our girls so they are used to saying them loudly and confidently, and they just roll off their tongue when required. This role-play need not be elaborate. When your daughter tells you about an incident of bad behaviour, ask her to think about what she said, what she could have said, and what she might say in similar cases in the future.

It sounds so simple, but a well-timed and well-delivered quick comeback can cut off poor behaviour at the knees. It lets the other child know that your daughter is not going to put up with what they've done and can also reduce the chances of it happening again. Research shows that kids who use the quick comeback technique tend to be teased less often and less severely than other children.[10]

The three magic words that resolve conflicts

Girls and women are often taught from an early age to avoid conflict at all costs. When someone doesn't agree with them or hurts their feelings, girls are told to either pretend it never happened, or minimise or distrust their own response. If that doesn't work, they can then be tempted to tear the other girl or woman down behind her back to make themselves feel better. While not rocking the boat might make for a quieter life, it means that these girls and women never develop the skills to resolve conflict with their friends – or anyone else. The phenomenon of ghosting, of ending a friendship abruptly and without explanation, shows just how much women detest conflict. When you have no ability to deal with friction, it's often less painful to completely cut off a friend, even one that you may have had for years, than to talk about the problem you have with her and try to resolve it.

But dealing with conflict is quite simple and straightforward once we know how to do it. Dana Kerford teaches three little words to resolve any conflict: 'When . . . I feel . . .'

Okay, okay, there are a few more words that you have to add after 'When' and 'I feel'. But this formula is the basis for starting to resolve any conflict. Your daughter calmly explains what the friend did that upset her and how it made her feel. For example, 'When you say I'm a baby because I bring my toy on camp, I feel sad,' or, 'When you always take King in four square and don't let others have a turn, it makes the game unfair and I don't like to play like that.'

The next step is for your daughter to pause and listen to what her friend has to say. The best outcome is that these words open up a space to discuss the conflict in a productive way. Of course, that's the ideal. Everything may not go according to plan. Your daughter's friend may have limited or no experience of dealing with friendship trouble as well. If your daughter's friend closes up or lashes out, there's a simple response to that too: 'I can see you're not ready to talk about this right now. Let me know when you are.'

Your daughter's friend may never come back to your daughter to have the conversation. Where conflict is concerned, there are no guaranteed happy endings. But at least your daughter tried to clear the air and repair her friendship. And she did so in a way that showed respect not only for herself by not putting up with hurtful behaviour, but also for the friendship by trying to resolve the conflict rather than letting it grow. Even knowing that you've tried to deal with the problem can feel empowering, regardless of the result.

This technique is obviously too complicated for very young girls. Some might think that it is even too sophisticated and mature for older girls. But we have seen it in action: girls who have role-played this script in Kerford's workshop, practised at home with their parents, and then successfully applied it in the schoolyard. Violet learned these conflict-resolution skills when she was seven and has used them to resolve disputes with her friends. She's now even using this approach with us!

Should we get involved in our kids' friendships conflicts?

There are times when you'll feel like the negotiating team for the United Nations. You may be tempted to schedule peace talks with other children's parents, or you may be asked to negotiate treaties and no-play zones on your kids' behalf. Our advice is to resist or, if you're the one being lobbied, give a firm no. Nothing good will come of it. Phoning other parents or marching up to the school demanding intervention often does more harm than good.

If your daughter thinks you're going to take matters into your own hands when she doesn't want you to, she may stop confiding in you. And even if she wants you to fight her battles for her, doing so may disempower her. Every time we step in to resolve our daughter's problems, we are effectively telling her that she is not capable of doing it herself. We are also denying her the opportunity to practise her social skills and build resilience. Rather than acting as lead negotiator in your daughter's relationships, support her and coach from the sidelines.

The first step in that process is to listen.

While listening seems so simple, it's often overlooked, probably for that very reason. Just as with adults, when your daughter talks about her problems she wants to feel heard, validated and understood. We need to remind ourselves that what might seem small to us can loom large in the eyes of our daughter.

The second step is to ask her, 'Did you stand up for yourself?' This makes it clear to your daughter that you expect her to confront conflict and bad behaviour instead of ignoring it or running away from it. If she didn't stand up for herself then that is a good opportunity to talk about – and even role-play – the steps of quick comebacks and conflict resolution that we outlined earlier (see page 162).

It can also be beneficial to ask questions that help your daughter work out if she needs to take further action to deal with the situation and how she can handle it better in the future. For example, 'Was your friend being mean on purpose or do you think it was an accident?' or, 'Do you think your friend understood that you didn't like what she did, or do you need to explain it to her?' or, 'What happened afterwards?' or, 'What do you think you will say next time you see her?' Then, as all good coaches would do, step back, cheer from the sidelines and tell your daughter, 'You've got this.'

What about bullying?

All of this advice is useful for garden-variety conflicts. But for bullying, you may need a different approach. There are times when the problem is too big and serious for a girl to deal with on her own.

We need to be clear about what bullying is and what it isn't. Bullying is a word that is often misused. It can be thrown around loosely, applied to situations and behaviours that, while not desirable, are not bullying. A child not wanting to play with your daughter at lunchtime is not bullying. A child taking your daughter's pencil is not bullying. A child accidentally bumping into your daughter in the corridor is not bullying. None of these is pleasant but they are not bullying and are most likely situations that your daughter can learn to manage on her own, with your support and encouragement.

Bullying is when a child is deliberately and repeatedly seeking to harm, intimidate or coerce your daughter. If your daughter has tried the quick comeback and the conflict-resolution strategies and a child continues to cause deliberate harm, then it's time for the adults to get involved. It is our responsibility to make sure that children feel safe and supported. In a school, preschool or child-care environment this means speaking to the leadership team and working out a plan that both you and your daughter are comfortable with. In social situations it may mean not visiting certain friends anymore so that your daughter is not put at risk.

It may mean cultivating a wider friendship network for your daughter. Signe Whitson says that one of the simplest and most powerfully protective strategies parents can use to minimise the impact of bullying is to seek out opportunities for their kids to form positive peer relationships outside of school. It could be through an extracurricular activity, a sporting team, a family friend or a relative. What's important is that these friendships exist outside of the dynamic of school or preschool, so that if your daughter is feeling excluded there at any time she will not feel friendless. She'll have a tangible support network that makes her feel validated. You may have to deliberately encourage and foster these friendships outside of school and preschool, but the investment will pay off by ensuring your daughter won't ever feel totally rejected and alone.

What if your child is the bully?

We have heard countless stories over the years about children being bullied. But the number of times a parent has told either of us that their child has bullied others can be counted on one hand. Our friend who was told by her daughter's teacher that her daughter was bullying other children was completely shocked by the news. She felt humiliated, frustrated and helpless.

While most of us don't like to think about it, some of our kids are going to bully other children.

The warning signs that your daughter might be bullying another child is if she is not being invited to birthday parties or playdates, or if she demonstrates exclusive and domineering behaviour towards a friend, or if she has very few genuine friends. Dana Kerford says, 'Other signs are if your child has misplaced confidence, [is] putting on a mask or front to give off the "king of the castle" vibe or exhibiting relational aggression or physical aggression when frustrated.' Kerford says that the best approach to curb this kind of behaviour is for other children to govern it on their own, by standing up to bullies and not tolerating their bad behaviour. However, parents and teachers need to follow up with consequences as well.

Forcing a child to simply apologise is insufficient, as a child who is attention-seeking will find this rewarding. Therefore, it's important that parents choose a consequence that will discourage their daughter from doing it again. While immediate, logical consequences that match the behaviour are necessary, not being invited to birthday parties or playdates also serves as a natural repercussion of unkind behaviour. As heartbreaking as it sometimes is, helping your child recognise there are consequences for their actions is essential in changing negative behaviour patterns.

Parents also need to address the root cause of the behaviour. It's highly unlikely that any girl would wake up one day and set her sights on being a bully. It's more likely that something happened as a result of a number of experiences that led to her choosing inappropriate actions.

'Children with big, explosive emotions need guidance and support to find strategies to calm themselves down. The key for parents is to recognise when their child is starting to feel angst, like a balloon blowing up with air,' says Kerford. 'The goal is to help their child prevent the balloon from popping by giving their child very practical, step-by-step ideas to work their way through the emotion.'

Strengthening your daughter's empathy can also help. Empathy is a skill and, with practice, she can learn to be empathetic. 'It takes some children a long time to cognitively be capable of seeing outside of themselves. You can help your child with this by getting them to make the connection between how their actions affect others,' says Kerford. 'Asking them, "How do you think Sally felt when you said she was being a baby? What if someone called you a baby? How would that make you feel?" helps them to strengthen those empathy muscles.'

It would be tempting to ignore your daughter's bullying behaviour and simply refuse to believe she would be capable of being mean on purpose. But denial will not enable the development of the strong and meaningful friendships that a girl who likes herself needs. If you are willing to recognise that your daughter is bullying, then you can take steps to address it and help her change this behaviour by teaching her the emotional and social skills required to make friends.

Strengthening relationships with trusted adults

During the early years of your daughter's life, it's likely you will be the person she confides in. Yours will be the voice she listens to and trusts most. But this won't always be the case. As our daughters grow and discover their own identities, it is natural for them to want to rebel and separate themselves from us. In fact, there will be times when ours will be the last advice they want to take. There may also be times when they feel that they can't confide in us even though they want to. Teenage girls often report that they feel that their parents are too busy or too judgemental to actually listen to them.[11]

Looking ahead, when our daughters will go through these periods of not wanting to (or feeling that they can't) confide in us – for whatever reason – we want them to be confiding in a trusted adult instead. We're talking about a person who is wiser and older than they are, who shares our values and has our daughters' best interests at heart. We want this to be someone who will listen, support them and give good advice. A trusted adult is also a positive role model to whom your daughter can look for inspiration and guidance.

In previous generations, this person might have been a grandmother, an aunt or, depending on culture and religion, a figure like a godmother. But many people now live far away from their birth family, or have complex family structures, or different values, so this traditional set-up may no longer be possible, practical or desirable. You may need to deliberately cultivate the relationships that previously were filled by the grandmother/aunty/godmother figure.

Think carefully about the adults in your life and who among them would make good trusted friends for your daughter. Make sure you choose people who are going to be around for the long haul. A trusted adult has to be a stable and consistent part of your daughter's life. Other than a grandmother, an aunty or a godmother, they could be a coach, a neighbour or a close friend.

You don't want to leave such an important relationship to chance, so make it official. Ask those people if they are willing to fill that role in your daughter's life. Explain that you want them to help support and guide your daughter as she grows into a woman, so they know that being a trusted adult is an honour and a responsibility. To maximise the chances of your daughter turning to the trusted adult in a crisis, make sure she develops a bond with them as early as possible. We see trusted adult relationships a bit like insurance policies. If we spend time nurturing the connection while our daughters are young (when the relationships are not absolutely essential), they are more likely to turn to that person when they are older.

In a world where many girls look to social media as a template for successful and idealised womanhood, the need for positive role models has never been so great. Parenting author Maggie Dent takes her role as a trusted adult very seriously, saying, 'A young woman can't be what she hasn't seen, so aunties can expand her vision, rather than her relying on bloggers and celebrities to inform that.'[12]

Trusted adults and confidentiality

One of the most important roles that the trusted adult plays is to be someone your daughter can speak to in complete confidence. This means that, whoever you pick, they need to be able to keep your daughter's secrets if she asks them to. Yes, that includes from you. Actually, it means keeping her secrets especially from you.

Let us explain. Kids withhold information from their parents for all sorts of reasons. Sometimes they're afraid that they might get into trouble. In these situations, one of the biggest barriers to your daughter confiding in a trusted adult is the fear that that person will tell you. In other cases, more worryingly, a common tactic of predators (both online and off) is frightening kids into keeping what's going on from their parents. Abuse of all kinds – sexual, emotional and psychological – often goes on for years because the predator has told the child that they are not to tell their parents.

We've seen firsthand just how easily children can be scared into keeping secrets from their parents. When Violet went off to grade four camp, her friends shared scary stories about Momo, an internet phenomenon. Momo is an evil-looking, manga-like character with contorted bird features, who is said to have supernatural powers to possess and even kill children. According to the stories told by Violet's schoolmates, Momo has hypnotic powers and can hide in children's cupboards and make them do evil deeds; and if a child tells their parents about Momo, the creature will kill their parents.

Most of the kids on Violet's school camp had never seen a Momo video. The extent of Momo's influence across YouTube is exaggerated. But none of that mattered to these kids. Just hearing the stories was enough to frighten them. Some of the children in Violet's class returned from camp clearly distraught but refused to tell their parents the reason for their distress because they honestly believed that if they did Momo would kill their mum.

While Momo presented no real danger to these children, it was astonishing to see how easily these eight- and nine-year-olds could be manipulated into keeping secrets from their parents. We are quite sure that other parents have told their kids that they can talk to them about anything, just as we have done countless times. But in the heat of the moment, all those reassuring words meant nothing. They failed at the very first hurdle.

Violet did eventually tell us about the Momo stories. We thanked her and praised her for having the courage to speak to us. Then we used the situation to remind her that at any time she can talk to one of her trusted adults and, if she requests it, they will not tell us.

You need to make sure your daughter knows that if she's ever in trouble where she feels she can't tell you, then she can talk to a trusted adult and the trusted adult will only tell you with your daughter's permission. In our family, the trusted adult will encourage our daughter to tell us what's going on if it's serious. But if she doesn't want us to know, then our friend has promised to keep it confidential. Our daughters understand this. And the trusted adult knows this and agrees to it.

Of course we would prefer to know. The idea of either of our daughters struggling with a serious issue that we aren't aware of is frightening beyond words. Yet so much worse than us not knowing would be our daughter not getting the help and support she needs from an adult with good values.

While we are under no illusion that this is a bulletproof strategy, it's one more way in which we can try to protect our daughters. Our hope is that this arrangement will give them the courage to speak to a trusted adult, rather than feel that they need to deal with a big problem on their own. If nothing else, it provides our daughters with someone they can go to when life – or their parents – becomes too much.

Strengthening your relationship with your daughter

Studies of lottery winners find a pretty consistent pattern. After they experience an initial spike in happiness, they soon return to their habitual mood from before they became fabulously wealthy.[13] More *stuff* – material stuff – doesn't seem to do much for our long-term happiness. The research is very clear on what does work. As neuroscientist Dr Sarah McKay outlines in her excellent book *The Women's Brain Book*, there are many, many studies that show it is human connection, love and affection that will strengthen your daughter's wellbeing, both now and throughout her whole life.[14] This also applies to your relationship with your daughter. Giving her more stuff will only give her a temporary high. What she craves is a connection – a deep and meaningful connection with you.

You're busy, right? We get it. At the end of a long day we're tired and can easily fall into a trap where the most interaction we have with our girls is telling them to clean their teeth, put their shoes away or stop bickering with each other. But our daughters need to feel connected with us almost as much as they need to breathe.

The good news is that there is a way to strengthen your bond with your daughter even when you're time-poor and exhausted. It turns out that, when it comes to developing and maintaining a strong and happy relationship, how you celebrate good news is where it counts.[15] Psychology professor Shelly Gable from the University of California discovered that how you celebrate is perhaps more important for your relationship than how you fight or deal with conflict. It's all about asking the right questions, in the right way, at the right (happy) times.

Here's how it works. When your daughter comes to you with some good news or an achievement of some sort, stop what you're doing, smile, give her a hug and ask her a question about it.

There. That's it. It really is as simple as that.

Social scientists like Gable have a fancy name for this. It's called an 'active and constructive' response. Active and constructive responses have three ingredients: they are authentic, enthusiastic and supportive. They contrast with 'passive and constructive' responses, such as saying something like, 'That's great. Well done,' while you're transfixed by your phone or the telly.

Then there are destructive ways to respond. For example, an 'active and destructive' response to the news that your daughter has been voted class captain might be, 'That sounds like a lot of responsibility. Are you sure you're up for it? What will your friends think about you bossing them around?' Finally, 'passive and destructive' responses are statements like, 'I'm busy right now. Not everything revolves around you,' said while you stare at your phone or computer screen.

It takes five minutes, or probably even less, to give your daughter an active and constructive response. Put down your phone or stop chopping the carrots, look your daughter in the eye, and ask her a few questions to show that you are interested and excited about her happy news. You will bank some major parent–daughter relationship credit.

Action for dads

Take a day of annual leave to go on your daughter's school, preschool or childcare excursion or to be a parent helper. If there aren't formal opportunities to do this, ask your daughter's teacher if you can come in and read the class a story or help with another activity.

A study published in 2018 in the *Journal of Marriage and Family* found that children with fathers who spend time engaged in educational activities experience a great deal of cognitive benefits, as compared to fathers who engage in other structured activities such as sports and unstructured activities such as play. Best of all, this applies regardless of your own academic achievements.[16]

The benefits of taking a day off to get involved in your daughter's education extend far beyond academic pursuits. With just one little annual leave day, you will be able to meet all your daughter's friends and witness firsthand how she interacts with them. If you see that she needs assistance developing her social skills, you can offer it. Knowing your daughter's friends (and their names) provides an opportunity to open up communication about those relationships. If she comes to you looking for advice in the future about an issue with a friend, you will know immediately who she's talking about.

Additionally, spending that day with your daughter will allow you to have a one-on-one chat with her teacher. It will also show your daughter that you are genuinely interested in her life and what's important to her.

Recap

- Girls who have strong and meaningful relationships are physically and emotionally healthier, have a greater sense of wellbeing, do better at school, are more resilient and assertive and go on to be more successful professionally.
- It is a myth that social skills and friendship skills develop naturally. Your daughter may need specific instructions about how to make eye contact, make conversation, choose quality friends and deal with conflict in a productive way. The good news is that these skills can be taught and practised just like any other.
- Invest early in building your daughter's support crew. Choose a select number of trusted adults who share the same values as you and ask them to be your daughter's trusted adults now and into the future. Nurture these relationships now so that when your daughter is older, she will hopefully turn to one of her trusted adults for advice, rather than a peer or a celebrity or social media.

- Your daughter is desperate for a deep and meaningful connection with you. Bang-for-buck connection strategies include devoting uninterrupted time to celebrate and show an interest in her successes, and taking one little annual leave day each year to be a classroom helper – to meet her teacher, get to know her friends and show your daughter that she's a priority.

7

A girl who likes
herself is herself

Stone parenting vs seed parenting

Every other week the media seems to serve up a new parenting style. There are tiger parents, helicopter parents, snowplow parents, lawnmower parents, ride-on-lawnmower parents. Actually, we made that last one up but you get the picture. At the risk of adding to the already too-long list of parenting styles, allow us to suggest two more: stone parenting and seed parenting.

Stone parenting and seed parenting relate to how parents view the task of raising children. Stone parents see their child as a column of precious marble. In this approach, the role of the parent is to chip away at the marble, to sculpt and mould the child, bringing forth a masterpiece. Stone parents believe that the child has certain qualities, but that the parents should decide what shape and direction the child will take. Some parents may want to sculpt a 'mini-me' daughter; others may want to raise a girl who is the complete opposite of themselves. Either way, it is the parents who are wielding the chisel.

In contrast, seed parents view their children as, you guessed it, seeds to be nurtured and grown. These parents see their job as providing the best possible environment for their seed to sprout and then bloom: they supply the fertile soil, nutrients and the trellis against which the child can lean on to grow, but they ultimately let the sapling develop in its own time and in its own way. The environment the parents provide influences the process and the result, but it is the child who ultimately determines what shape they will take and in which direction they will grow.

Both stone and seed parents are motivated by love and want what is best for their daughter. The difference is that stone parents think that the best outcome for their daughter comes from external influences such as themselves, grandparents, schools or coaches, social expectations or tradition – or some combination of these. Seed parents, in contrast, see growing up as a more organic and intrinsic process. They trust their daughter to develop when and how she is meant to.

It's likely that most of us combine a little bit of each approach. Or in some contexts we'll tend towards stone parenting, while in others we'll lean towards seed parenting. But we may have a dominant approach or inclination for one style of parenting over the other.

We started off as stone parents without knowing it. We read all the books and brochures about developmental milestones and meticulously studied the charts that plotted Violet's progress against averages. We thought it was our role as 'good' parents to push her as far and as fast as we could. We had fallen for the idea that parenting is a competitive sport, and we didn't want our daughter to get left behind. Naturally, we also wanted what was best for her, and assumed that our approach was the correct one.

But as time went by, as we became more confident parents, we realised that Violet was her own unique and wonderful person. If we tried to force her into our vision for her, we would be denying her the opportunity to discover her true, authentic self. We've since learned that a girl who likes herself has to be allowed to grow into the best version of the person *she* chooses to be, not a version of herself that is chosen for her, no matter how well intentioned. So we now try to keep our stone parenting inclinations in check. We do our best to put down our chisels and pick up our watering cans.

In this chapter we're going to explore how we can enable girls to discover, develop and like their authentic selves. We'll look at ways that you can nurture your daughter so that she flourishes throughout her life.

Allow her strengths to blossom

'What are her strengths?' Violet's grade three teacher asked us.

We were squished into the small moulded plastic chairs in the classroom, the faint yet permanent smell of school-lunches-past in the air. It was a ten-minute meet-and-greet session for parents to talk to their child's teacher, without their children present, about any relevant issues for the upcoming year. We were expecting to discuss everything from the maths and English curricula, to friendship concerns, to any emotional or behavioural issues. We weren't expecting Violet's teacher to ask about her strengths. In fact, it was the first time in our eight years of parenting that we had been asked that question. And it was so unexpected that, for a moment or two, we had to think.

It turns out we weren't alone in being caught off-guard by the teacher's question. A number of friends later told us they drew a blank during their meetings. Even with prompting and awkward silences, they couldn't come up with a single strength for their child.

Psychology professor Lea Waters says that it's common for parents to struggle to list their child's strengths. Professor Waters runs workshops on strength-based parenting, which explain the benefits of focusing on children's strengths rather than always trying to correct their weaknesses. She has observed that parents in her workshops often have a hard time coming up with more than a few strengths for their children. Keep in mind that these parents have paid and signed up for a course on strength-based parenting, so, unlike our meet-and-greet session with the teacher, they presumably had already had a chance to think about where their child's strengths might lie. Still, they are often stumped by the question. It's not that their kids don't have strengths. They absolutely do. It's just that we parents don't tend to notice them.

Why is it that many parents can easily list their daughter's weaknesses, issues and problems, and yet flounder when it comes to naming what she does well?

Part of the answer to that question may lie in how we were parented ourselves. In the past, a common parenting style was 'corrective parenting'. Parents saw their main task as fixing weaknesses. They effectively tried to chisel off and 'correct' the parts of their child that they presumed would prevent them from becoming successful adults.

Another reason is that we are so focused on looking out for signs that our child is falling behind that we neglect to notice what they're good – or even great – at. 'At a basic biological level, even though we love our children, our brains are wired to avoid what's going wrong before we notice what's going right,' says Professor Waters, author of *The Strength Switch*. 'This means that we are more likely to notice the subjects that our children are struggling with at school rather than those that they excel at. Or we may reprimand them for rudeness, never noticing – much less crediting them – when they're being polite.'

But if parents are too busy concentrating on what is wrong with their daughter and directing their efforts into 'fixing' her faults – shaping her and crafting her to their standards – they won't have the time or the headspace to notice and nurture her unique gifts and talents. Just like the flyscreen game we talked about in the Power Perspective chapter, if parents spend most of their time focused on the flyscreen of their daughter's flaws, they may neglect to see the beauty and wonder beyond it.

This approach can affect the way your daughter perceives and feels about herself. If you focus too much on what's wrong with her, she may grow up feeling constantly inadequate. She may come to define herself by what she can't do, rather than by what she can. If your daughter feels she's failing all the time, she's unlikely to like herself.

'We mistakenly believe that the way to make our kids optimistic and resilient is to weed out all their weaknesses,' says Professor Waters. 'Strength-based science shows the opposite is true. It tells us to turn the bulk of our attention to expanding their strengths rather than reducing their weaknesses.'

Your daughter's strengths

We don't know you or your daughter, but we can say with iron-clad certainty that your daughter possesses strengths. In fact, she probably has a whole heap of them. It's just that some of her strengths may be hiding in plain sight. Psychologist Dr Peter Benson, who spent over fifty years researching youth development, said that every child has natural talents and interests that genuinely excite them, and that are good and useful to the world. He called this their 'spark'.[1] Your daughter's sparks are the pursuits that make her heart sing, the characteristics she genuinely likes about herself. Her sparks are the qualities or activities that she's naturally good at and chooses to do without nagging or prompting, and that energise her and fill her with joy.

Dr Benson's research showed that finding and nurturing that spark will give a girl purpose. When your daughter is working from her strengths, she is in touch with her authentic self – who she really is, not what the world thinks she should be. Unsurprisingly, this brings a whole raft of other benefits. Encouraging children to play to their strengths leads to greater levels of happiness and engagement at school, increased life satisfaction and self-esteem, higher academic achievement, and greater confidence and resilience. By recognising and cultivating your daughter's strengths, you will be building her up and helping her reach her potential without the nagging, the pushing and the chiselling.

The job of seed parents is to help your daughter recognise her strengths, and to nurture them and allow them to blossom in their right season.

Finding her strengths

If you're unsure what your daughter's strengths are, ask her. What does she love to do? What excites her? What does she feel so passionate about that when she gets onto the subject she won't stop talking about it? If she is unable to recognise or articulate her strengths, then observe her and her strengths may reveal themselves. Look out for something that your daughter is naturally good at, and that she chooses to use or do without prompting or pressure, and that energises her.

Professor Lea Waters warns parents not to confuse a skill with a strength. Think of the joyless piano player: the girl who has been *forced* to practise the piano every day since she was three. She may be a *skilful* player, but playing does not excite her or make her happy. She'd give it up tomorrow if her parents would let her, or if she hadn't learned to believe that not acing the next music exam would be a sign of failure.

If you're still struggling to identify your daughter's strengths, we've compiled a list of attributes in an appendix at the end of this book (see page 203). We're pretty sure that if you go through it, you'll find many strengths that apply to your daughter.

Nurturing her strengths

Once we've identified our daughters' strengths, the next step is to nurture and reinforce them. This can be as simple as acknowledging a strength whenever you see your daughter use it. '[I]f your children are sharing, you can thank them for their behaviour and say how you see them using a strength,' Professor Waters says. For example, 'Thanks for sharing with your sister – that's really kind (or fair) of you.' If your son has lost motivation to study for exams, you can remind him, 'Now's the time for your perseverance to come to the fore.'

The added benefit of focusing on your daughter's strengths is that it makes your job as a parent a little easier – not to mention more fun. With the constant pressure to be the best possible parents, raising the best possible girls, it's easy to get caught up in all the aspects of parenting at which you think you are failing. But when you focus on your daughter's strengths and see the beautiful, unique individual that you're raising, you will realise that you're actually doing a fine job after all.

Isn't this just an excuse for mediocrity?

While focusing on your daughter's strengths sounds lovely in theory, does it work in practice? Might it just mean that you end up viewing your daughter through rose-coloured glasses, concentrating on her positives while overlooking important areas where she's struggling or even falling behind? If your daughter is finding reading difficult, for example, do you really have the luxury of focusing on the positives?

'It's not about ignoring the fact that they can't read,' says Professor Waters. 'It's about giving them help where they need it but also seeing that one fault within the larger kaleidoscope of your child.' It may sound counterintuitive, but focusing on your daughter's strengths can help her to better address areas where she may be weak. 'When a child is not defining themselves by what's missing, they're able to say, "Well, I know I'm not a good reader and I'm getting extra help with that, but I am a good basketballer or I'm creative, or I can figure out computers easily."' If your daughter sees herself as a constant failure, then addressing weakness can be crushing. Whereas if you have helped her realise and develop all of her natural and positive characteristics, then she will be stronger and more robust when she works on the skills she struggles with.

Praise does not cancel out criticism

Spend more time noticing and remarking on what your daughter is doing right rather than what she is doing wrong. Psychology professor Suniya Luthar says that parents often make the mistake of thinking that their criticism of their child can be balanced out by their praise of their child's achievements and by giving them lots of affection. This is not the case. When it comes to impact and longevity, criticism trumps praise every time. 'Praise does not cancel out criticism,' says Professor Luthar. 'Psychologists have firmly established that disparaging words or attitudes have a much stronger impact than words of praise, by at least a factor of three.'

How do you feel when you're criticised? Not great, huh? Does it motivate you? Does it make you feel loved and valued and inspired? If you're like most of us, the answer is no. As adults, we can often walk away from criticism as we are better equipped to put it into perspective. Children can't do this with their parents' criticism. Of course we need to guide and correct our kids, but this can be done without shredding them with criticism. Be the trellis, not the chisel. Think back to your daughter's little card of special people whose opinions she can trust and value from chapter one. It's more than likely your name is there. Your words have tremendous power.

The 'Good Girl' Syndrome

With all this talk of strengths, we need to make something emphatically clear. While your daughter's strengths will most likely need nurturing and developing, they already reside within her. They are part of her authentic self, who she really is. They are not necessarily what you or the rest of the world thinks she should be.

There is a long history of girls and women being praised for qualities such as sweetness, niceness, compliance, prettiness, and being constantly obliging and self-sacrificing. While some of these qualities may be your daughter's natural strengths (that energise her and give her joy), very often nurturing them in a girl benefits people other than her. This is the difference between developing a girl's strengths and manipulating her into being a 'Good Girl'.

'What's so bad about being a Good Girl?' you might be wondering. The short answer is: everything. A Good Girl is the exact opposite of a girl who is herself.

Before you slam this book shut to fling it across the room in confusion or frustration, let's have a little pop quiz.

1. When you meet someone, do you wonder, 'Will they like me?' before you think, 'Will I like them?'
2. If you disagree with someone, do you worry that that person will no longer like you?
3. Would you rather lie to be nice than tell the truth and risk being disagreeable?
4. If someone asks, 'Do you want a cup of tea?', do you find yourself saying something like, 'Oh, no. Well, okay, but only if you're having one'?
5. If someone offers to pick your daughter up from school, do you say something like, 'No, it's okay. I wouldn't want to inconvenience you. And look! The rain is starting to ease'?
6. If someone offers you the last piece of cake, do you decline and tell them to save it for someone else?

If you answered yes to a couple of these questions, it's likely you've got a touch of the Good Girl Syndrome. If you found yourself nodding in furious agreement to most of them, then chances are you've got a full-blown case of Good Girlitis.

A Good Girl is an unfailing people-pleaser who feels like she must be selfless, obliging and get along with everybody, no matter how she's treated. She is unerringly nice and bites her tongue rather than risk making someone uncomfortable. She smiles when she's sad, laughs when she's angry and drops hints instead of asking for what she wants. She won't put anyone out on her account. To phrase it another way, Good Girls are saying to the world, 'I'm not worth it. You must have something better to do with your time/food/small change than give it to me.'

Being a Good Girl is not really about being a good person. In fact, being a Good Girl is not really about being 'good' at all. It's about being compliant and subservient, and trying to measure up to some impossible ideal set up by someone else. The Good Girl Syndrome forces girls and women into a straitjacket of sweetness and light where they must ignore their needs and repress their feelings. It's about girls performing for others, conforming to suffocating expectations, putting others' needs ahead of their own. Good Girls, in short, are not themselves.

Raising a Good Girl is an extreme form of stone parenting because her authentic self is sanded away, hidden from the world so that all that is left is sweet, obliging graciousness. Good girls aren't permitted to feel – and don't permit themselves to feel – jealousy or anger. They aren't allowed to be critical or self-centred. While we might wish it were otherwise, all these traits are part of the human condition. Raising a girl with the expectation that she should never upset anyone is setting her up to feel like she is never good enough. Occasionally disagreeing with others, disappointing them and, yes, being in conflict with them is part of what makes us fully rounded human beings.

The constant effort of maintaining the facade of the Good Girl is corrosive to a girl's character. When girls do eventually experience those 'unacceptable' emotions (as they inevitably will because of that pesky condition called 'being human') they often turn on themselves in the form of feeling shame and self-loathing.

As Rachel Simmons, author of *The Curse of the Good Girl*, writes, 'Good Girl pressure delivers a sucker punch to girls' emotional intelligence . . . When girls cannot identify, express, and accept a full range of their feelings, they lose critical connections to themselves and their relationships.'[2] Simmons says that girls who aspire to the impossible standards set by the Good Girl model are ruthlessly hard on themselves. They can be crushed by a little mistake and take any sort of feedback too personally.

The pressure to be a Good Girl is a wolf in sheep's clothing that is devouring our daughters from the inside out. It's simply not possible for anyone, no matter how sweet their nature is, to please everyone all the time. Since Good Girls are expected to choose social harmony over conflict, their unresolved and unexpressed frustration festers inside them until it finds a way out, usually in the form of self-destructive behaviour. 'The distress of young girls is clearly visible in the rising rates of mental health problems, binge drinking, eating disorders and the rampant growth of bullying in our schools,' writes Kate Figes, author of *The Terrible Teens*. 'Girls are now expected to be all things – attractive, thin, good, successful, happy, kind, loving, self-sufficient; perfect, in other words.'[3]

This incapacity of Good Girls and the women they become to prioritise their own needs has consequences that go beyond relatively trivial acts (such as declining the offer of a cup of tea) and last much longer. It affects friendships, romantic relationships and professional success. As Simmons notes, 'The Curse of the Good Girl erects a psychological glass ceiling that begins its destructive sprawl in girlhood and extends across the female life span, stunting the growth of skills and habits essential to becoming a strong woman.'

This isn't just some quirky behaviour women engage in. From the time they are toddlers, girls are rewarded for being Good Girls – and punished when they don't stick to the Good Girl script. We have a whole dictionary of words that are used to label girls who express themselves authentically and say what they think. 'Bossy', 'opinionated', 'selfish', 'difficult', 'aggressive', 'bitchy' and worse are all applied to girls who let slip that they have opinions.

Don't get us wrong: our opposition to raising Good Girls is not about allowing our girls to behave like feral terrors or excusing bad behaviour. Nor are we saying that parents shouldn't have rules and standards. They absolutely should. We are big believers in strong boundaries and high expectations. What we are advocating for is allowing girls to grow into fully rounded human beings rather than one-dimensional cut-outs who perform for everyone else. Instead of raising Good Girls, our aim should be raising Real Girls.

How to raise a Real Girl

Ask and you might receive; hint and you definitely won't

In our first chapter we wrote about the importance of encouraging girls to ask for what they want rather than hinting, because hinting makes them passive and prevents them from taking charge of their lives. The reluctance or inability of girls and women to ask for what they want is also a key symptom of the Good Girl Syndrome. Instead of feeling entitled to prioritise their own needs and desires, Good Girls drop hints and hope other people will guess, or else they miss out on getting what they want entirely.

A lot of grown women have problems asking for what they want. For example, we have friends who leave product catalogues featuring gifts that they want lying around the house in the lead-up to their birthdays, and who are then inevitably disappointed when their 'hints' fly under everyone's radar. We have single friends who won't ask a man out on a date because they fear being considered 'too forward' – whatever that means in the twenty-first century. Another friend who works in marketing told us about a focus group she ran with thirty-something women. As this was a focus group, its express purpose was to find out these women's preferences and opinions. But even here, these women were only able to articulate their preferences through their children or partner. Rather than saying what they liked, they would answer, 'My son would like this,' or, 'My husband would enjoy that.'

These women were all performing the Good Girl script: they couldn't express what they thought or make clear what they wanted for fear of being seen as selfish or unfeminine. For women in our culture, asking for what you want is a skill that needs to be nurtured and grown. You can help your daughter develop this skill by insisting that she asks for what she wants. This means actually naming it and owning it. We tell our girls, 'If you don't ask, you don't get.'

Teaching girls to say 'yes' as well as 'no'

We hear a lot about the importance of teaching girls that it's okay to say 'no'. Say 'no' to peer pressure, 'no' to unwanted sexual advances, 'no' to people who want to dominate, objectify or exploit you. But what about teaching girls to say 'yes'? Good Girls often struggle to say 'yes' because they don't want to impose on anyone or put anyone out. But if girls are not well practised in saying 'yes', they will miss out on countless opportunities throughout life.

After an interaction with our neighbour, we realised that we must explicitly teach our girls that 'It's okay to say YES!' or they would never learn it. When Violet was six she was saving up to buy a special book. One day our neighbour offered Violet some coins for her moneybox. Our neighbour knew that Violet was saving and this was her way of encouraging Violet's reading. Rather than accepting the money, Violet said, 'Oh, it's okay.'

Afterwards we asked Violet if she had actually wanted the coins. Of course she had! There was no reason why she wouldn't have wanted them. When we asked her why she didn't take the money, she shrugged and said she didn't know.

But we knew. She learned it from watching all the women in our family. When anybody offers them anything – no matter how big, small, necessary or frivolous – their immediate response is to decline. Good Girls are taught from an early age not to be greedy or selfish, nor to impose on or inconvenience anyone. To be a 'taker' rather than a 'giver' is just so unladylike. Money and food are particular areas where girls and women are rewarded for saying 'no'.

This unwillingness to accept offers of help, gifts, compliments, acknowledgement, or pretty much anything really, can have serious consequences for women's financial security and for their quality of life. It can mean the difference between drowning and being pulled ashore.

There will be enough people in your daughter's life who will imply she is less important and less worthy simply because of her gender. Developing an aversion to saying 'yes' will only reinforce this belief, and see her miss out on even more opportunities.

We told Violet that rudeness is about being inconsiderate or deliberately hurtful. It's not rude to prioritise her own needs and wants. If she is offered something that she would like, then all she has to do is look the person in the eye and say, 'Yes, please.'

The next time we saw our neighbour, she again asked Violet if she would like some money for her moneybox. This time Violet said 'yes' and walked away beaming with a fist full of five and ten cent coins, and, hopefully, a sense of self-worth. We now make a conscious effort to encourage our girls to say 'yes'.

Make the most of meltdowns

A Good Girl feels like she must always be joyful and sweet. She is not allowed to be angry, jealous, frustrated, or outwardly competitive. But given that these are natural human emotions, it is inevitable that your daughter is going to experience all of these, and more. If a girl grows up believing that these normal emotions are wrong and should be suppressed, she will likely feel fraudulent and ashamed every time she experiences them. This is going to make it tough for her to like herself. Rather than trying – and inevitably failing – to prevent our girls from experiencing these difficult yet authentic emotions, it's better to give them permission to feel them so they get lots of practice learning how to deal with them. We've found that tantrums are a great training ground for this.

When we were on our parenting L-plates, we were advised by numerous 'experts' – including doctors, maternal health nurses, teachers and other parents – that distraction was the best strategy to apply during tantrums. For example, if one of our daughters was cracking it over a broken toy, we should wave a different toy in front of her in the hope she'd forget all about being upset and move on to playing with the new distraction. If she was upset by another child or situation, then we should sing a song, do a dance or bounce her on our knee to shift her focus from the negative feeling onto something novel and less painful.

It's hard to watch your children suffer, especially when you know you could do something to alleviate it. It's like a knife to the heart. The distraction technique is tempting. There are times when you feel judged and embarrassed by your child's emotional display and you just want to shut them up as quickly as possible. In these situations, distraction may be the best approach for all concerned. But in general, distracting your daughter from her emotions means short-term gain for long-term pain, setting both parents and child up for failure.

The distraction technique is an example of stone parent-ing because it is effectively making the decision for your child about what they should and should not feel. It also denies girls the opportunity to learn how to deal with disappointment, anger or frustration and resolve their own emotions. Distracting kids is also a way of negating their feelings. In *The Whole-brain Child*, Daniel Siegel and Tina Payne Bryson write that the distraction approach can leave your child confused: 'He is still full of big and scary emotions, but he isn't allowed to deal with them in an effective way.[4]

A better option is to allow your daughter to experience her emotions, sympathise as necessary and, if she's willing, cuddle her while she cries out her difficult feelings. In this way, you can validate her emotions and her right to feel them. Think about how you feel after you allow your emotions to run their course and you have a good cry. You feel a lot better, right? Dealing with negative emotions is a process: you feel the pain, you express the pain (cry, call a friend, go for a walk), and then you resolve the pain and feel better. If we intervene and distract our girls from their authentic feelings, we are denying them the opportunity to complete the emotional process and feel the subsequent relief. We are also inadvertently teaching them that these feelings are wrong. It follows that they will feel wrong and ashamed when they experience emotions like disappointment, rage or frustration in the future.

You may be thinking that children are far too young to deal with these kinds of negative emotions. But ask yourself, at what age are they old enough to manage their emotions themselves? At what point do we as parents cut the cord? And, when you do cut the cord, if they haven't been given chances to practise dealing with emotions with your support, then how likely is it that they will work it out on their own? Wouldn't it be better to enable our girls to develop coping skills when we are there to help them, and when the stakes are lower?

A time and a place

If that all sounds like Hippie-dippie Parenting 101 – where children are rewarded for poor behaviour, allowing them to grow into self-centred emotional wrecks who yell and scream as they please – know that letting them express themselves isn't a licence to dominate everyone's time, attention and energy. You can still insist that your daughter express emotions in a way that does not become a means of getting everyone's attention. This is particularly applicable as your daughter gets older and is better able to manage her own emotions. As actress Kristen Bell tells her children when they are having a meltdown, 'You are allowed to be angry – that's okay. But you cannot be angry and sad in the middle of the living room while we're having dinner. You're welcome to go up to your bedroom and cry, but you're not allowed to ruin everybody else's evening because you're having a tantrum.'[5]

Just as important is that when your daughter feels better, she can rejoin you and feel welcomed and loved. When our girls have a meltdown, we don't distract them or get cross at them. First we make the best judgement we can about how much comfort they need from us, depending on the severity of the situation and the type and intensity of their emotions. For example, are they genuinely losing their shit or are they putting it on as a strategy to get their own way? We then calmly tell them to have their tantrum in their bedroom and then come back when they are feeling better. When they return, we greet them with big smiles and a hug to show them that we are pleased to see them again and happy that they have made themselves feel better. This response allows our girls to experience overwhelming emotions, develop their own coping skills in a safe environment, and know that no matter how they feel, or what they say or do, they will never be rejected.

Love, no strings attached

When the tantrum has been quelled and the anger and emotion have subsided, there is the opportunity for forgiveness. In terms of raising a girl who likes herself, this is where the real pay-off of the tantrum comes in.

You see, Good Girls believe they must fit into someone else's vision of who they should be in order to be loved. They think that if they do not please their parents/grandparents/teachers/friends, they will not be loved. This may be an incorrect perception on their part, but to the girl it is real. Rightly or wrongly, she may believe that if she isn't constantly sweet, obliging and agreeable, she risks alienating those who are most important to her.

As parents we need to have an honest chat with ourselves about whether we allow our girls to be anything but good. How great is the penalty for non-compliance in your family? Do you withdraw your love when your daughter disappoints you? Do you give her the silent treatment, shame her or reject her when she disobeys you? If our girls are too afraid to defy or disappoint us as parents, how are they ever going to have the courage to stand up to peer pressure, sexual pressure, inappropriate behaviour from colleagues and bosses, or companies seeking to exploit them? 'The sickness of the good child is that they have no experience of other people being able to tolerate their badness,' says *The Book of Life*, produced by resilience and self-development organisation The School of Life. 'They have missed out a vital privilege accorded to the healthy child; that of being able to display envious, greedy, egomaniacal sides and yet be tolerated and loved nevertheless.'[6]

Raising a girl who is herself means encouraging girls to give priority to their own needs and feelings. We must help our daughters unlearn the belief that it is their role in life to make sure everybody else is happy. This may involve times when she has a meltdown, or when her behaviour disappoints us or infuriates us. At these times, it's crucial that she knows unequivocally that she is still loved and accepted. We need to teach her that we love her even when she behaves in a way we don't like. She can disobey us, disappoint us and embarrass us but our love will remain unaffected. She doesn't have to make us proud or be compliant to receive our love.

Child and family mental health expert Claire Orange says that from the earliest stages of our parenting, we need to separate the child's behaviour from the child themselves, and always reassure our child that we love them unconditionally. 'When a child's behaviour is unacceptable parents should say, "I don't like your behaviour, but I love you, let's work on this together,"' says Orange. By contrast, judging the child would be to shame them, give them the silent treatment or say something such as, 'You're a very naughty child,' or, 'When you behave like that no one's going to like you.'

When we forgive our daughter's poor behaviour, we demonstrate that we love her no matter what. As a wise friend tells her son on a regular basis, 'There is nothing you could do that I cannot forgive.' Not only does this open up communication channels between her and her child, it also gives him the life-affirming gift of unconditional love. Forgiveness can be hard sometimes, especially if our children embarrass us, frustrate us or hurt us. Their words and actions can wound us deeply. But even in our most painful moments, it pays to remember that we are the adult and they are still learning about themselves and figuring out this complex world we live in.

Speaking up

Have you heard the phrase, 'It's fine' or 'I'm fine'? It's often delivered through gritted teeth and a smile that doesn't quite reach the eyes. This and other similar phrases are Good Girl code for, 'You've treated me badly but I don't want to upset you, cause a scene or honour my own needs so I'm just going to lie.' If you answered 'yes' a lot in our Good Girl quiz earlier, this phrase probably just rolls off your tongue. It also most likely gnaws at your soul, because putting yourself last *all the damn time* takes a physical and emotional toll. But regardless of the toll, Good Girls often continue to say, 'It's fine,' when it's clearly not, because they don't know what else to say. They have never practised how to stand up for themselves when someone crosses their boundaries.

We have taught our girls another way to respond in these situations. Well, actually, they both learned it at childcare but we reinforce it at home. The phrase is: 'Stop it, I don't like it.' Their fantastic childcare teachers taught our girls to stand up straight (shoulders back, head high) and say the phrase in their 'Biggest Big-girl Voice' whenever someone does something to them that makes them uncomfortable. It is clear they feel wonderfully empowered every time they say it.

This phrase comes in handy whenever another child tries to snatch your daughter's toy, knock over her tower of blocks or push her off the swing. It is the perfect phrase for a young girl learning to be assertive without being rude or aggressive. This simple phrase is a way of teaching girls that they have a right to stand up for themselves, that they don't have to tolerate or walk away from bad behaviour. Now that Violet is older she has replaced 'Stop it, I don't like it' with different, more age-appropriate phrases. But the lesson of speaking up has been well learned.

Sharing

Like most parents, we are big on teaching our girls to share because we want them to be kind, empathetic and considerate. But we don't want them to grow up believing that they must always put themselves last. Very often this is exactly what Good Girls are encouraged to do. In teaching girls to share, we need to be careful not to make them think that they are required to give up too much in order to please someone else. We make this distinction by allowing our girls to choose what they will not share with anyone. For example, they never have to share their favourite soft toy. When our girls were younger and other children tried to play with their favourite toy, we stepped in and explained that that was their special toy and it wasn't for sharing. Our girls are now capable of saying this themselves. We also tell them that it is okay not to share other toys but they need to not take them to preschool or school and to put them away before their friends come over to play.

When one of our girls receives a lolly bag from a birthday party, we tell her that it is her decision if she wishes to share the lollies with her sister. We also point out that if she shares with her sister, her sister is more likely to share with her when she comes home from a party with a lolly bag.

Parent the child you have, not the one you wish for

You may be on board with the theory of raising a girl who is herself, but what happens if your daughter turns out to be wildly different from how you wished she would be? What if the strengths and interests and activities that energise her lie in a completely different direction to your own? Maybe you've always been a gifted athlete and you'd hoped your daughter would be the same, but she couldn't care less about sport. Or perhaps you're the bookish type, at home in the library, but your daughter will only tolerate a book for a minute or two before she starts fidgeting and wants to move. Maybe you're a social butterfly with countless friends and your daughter is an introvert who prefers her own company. Maybe you wanted to steer her towards maths and science because that's where the money and the job security are, but her interests seem to be in the fine arts. Or perhaps you wanted her to be nothing like you and she seems to have already learned all your habits and character traits. In these cases you might be tempted to pick up the chisel, to ignore her natural strengths or sparks and try to shape her into your vision of what you want her to be.

While we don't believe this is the best approach to raising a girl who likes herself, it is absolutely normal to feel like this. Claire Orange says that for many parents, not getting the child they wanted can be incredibly disappointing. The dirty little secret some parents feel they can't admit to anyone is that among the joy and wonder of becoming a parent there is also sadness. 'We've got to come to the realisation and expectation in parenting that it's an equal journey of celebration and grief,' says Orange. 'In the celebration of all those milestones is also grieving for what we wanted for that child that you might not get.'

If you want your daughter to grow up being herself – and liking who that is – you need to be honest with yourself. If you are suffering from grief, know that you are not the only one, and this does not make you a bad person or an inadequate parent. What's important isn't that you experience these emotions, it's how you deal with them. It's about acknowledging your true feelings so that you can then face your grief and move on. Orange says that if parents can't get over their grief and disappointment on their own, they should get professional help. This will not only make their life as parents more enjoyable, but also help them to accept and love their child unconditionally.

If you do not deal with your grief, then you and your child will be in for not just a rough patch, but a rough stretch. We have a friend who teaches at an all-girls school. Every year when it's time for the senior students to submit their university course preferences, she tells us that girls come to her office in tears, begging for her help. The girls' parents are forcing them to choose university courses that the parents think are best for the girls but that they don't want to do. One girl was being forced into law when all she ever wanted to do was become a kindergarten teacher. There is no doubt that a career in the law is better paid and has a higher status than early-years education, but surely it is preferable to raise a fulfilled teacher than a miserable lawyer.

Nobody knows for certain what percentage of a person's strengths is genetic and what percentage can be influenced by their environment. Some experts say it's probably 50/50, while others suggest it's 70 per cent genetic and 30 per cent environment, but what they all agree on is that strengths are a combination of both.[7] Our girls are not formless lumps of stone that we can mould any which way we want, as the extreme version of stone parenting would have it. Our children's strengths are an outcome of both nature and nurture.

Obviously, we're more likely to raise girls who like themselves if we as parents nurture what is natural for them. It is up to our daughters to decide for themselves who they are, what they love to do and what their purpose is in the world. Our job is to help them be the best version of the person they want to be.

Action for dads

Do activities with your daughter that she likes, not just the things that you like.

In her excellent book *Fathers and Daughters*, Madonna King notes that dads might come along to support their daughters rowing but far fewer turn up to netball.[8] Some dads will only attend or take an interest in their daughter's activities if they also happen to enjoy them. Remember: a strength isn't what you think is best for your daughter. It's the activity that she chooses to do and takes delight in, without prompting from you – or anyone else. If you only involve yourself in the parts of your daughter's life that you like, you are telling her that she is not lovable or interesting to you when she is her authentic self. In order to get your attention and affection, she must become more like you (and less like herself).

You don't want to make your daughter choose between being her true self and pretending to be someone she's not in order to win your love and attention. This can lead to two outcomes, and neither of them are great: she will either fake who she is, or she will seek the approval and acceptance she craves elsewhere.

Let your daughter know that you want to spend time with her because you love her, not because you happen to like the same activities.

Recap

- Parenting approaches can be separated into two categories: stone parenting and seed parenting. Stone parents view their daughter as a precious stone for them to chisel and sculpt into their vision of what she should be. Seed parents, by contrast, view their daughter as a seed, full of potential, and they see their job as providing the best environment for their seed to grow and flourish. Seed parents nurture their daughter's development but they ultimately trust their daughter to grow into the best version of herself. While both parenting approaches are motivated by love, in order for a girl to like herself she must be able to decide for herself who she wants to be and when she becomes it.

- In the daily grind of parenting, it's possible to become so focused on fixing your daughter's flaws that you neglect to notice and nurture her strengths. A strength is a quality, behaviour or activity that your daughter is naturally good at and chooses to do, and that gives her joy and fulfilment. Every girl has a unique and special collection of strengths. Girls who recognise their strengths and receive more attention for them than their flaws do better by almost every measure compared with girls who define themselves by their weaknesses.

- Raising a Good Girl – a girl who is always sweet, obliging and self-sacrificing – might make life easier right now but it will slowly chip away at her self-worth. For a girl to like herself she must be allowed to be her authentic self, and this means experiencing and expressing the full range of emotions, being able to speak up and stand up for herself, and not believing that she must please everyone all the time in order to be loved.

- You might not have the daughter you were expecting. Being disappointed that she does not always meet your hopes, dreams and expectations is natural and normal. It does not make you a bad person or a bad parent to feel this way. But for the sake of your daughter, you need to work through your grief so you are better able to love and nurture the beautiful, wonderful, unique daughter you do have.

Final thoughts

Is it really possible to raise girls who like themselves? Can we spare our daughters from the self-hatred and self-doubt that are so often instilled in girls?

Looking around the world, many would believe that it is unlikely. Certainly, the odds are against us. There are so many toxic influences out of our control. Still, we're not going to go down without a fight.

What we all have is the power to control how *we* treat our girls. No matter what they face out in the world, we can choose to be their safe haven and their beacon, guiding them in discovering the wonderful, unique person they were born to be.

With our influence and support, our girls can grow up knowing that they are good enough just the way they are: we love them for who they are, not what they have achieved, what they wear or how much they weigh. We can give them the freedom to make mistakes, explore different identities, express their emotions and be authentic. We can give them the assurance that we will always have their back. We will love them because they are *them*.

Tell this to your daughter. Tell her again. And most of all, live it and keep living it.

That is what matters beyond all else.

Appendix

It's not always easy to put your daughter's strengths into words. While we may be able to see these strengths in action, parents often struggle to name them. This can make it difficult to praise and nurture those strengths. Instead, we revert to focusing on our daughters' weaknesses and shortcomings. The following is a list of strengths that we have gathered and adapted from Strengths Profile,[1] Angela Duckworth,[2] and the Values in Action Inventory of Strengths.[3]

Take a look and identify the beautiful, unique combination that your daughter possesses.

1. Ability to inspire and motivate others
2. Adaptability
3. Alternative perspectives
4. Appreciation of beauty
5. Artistic expression
6. Authenticity
7. Bounce-back
8. Bravery
9. Caution
10. Compassion
11. Competitive spirit
12. Confidence
13. Conscientiousness
14. Courage
15. Creativity
16. Curiosity
17. Dependability
18. Desire to help
19. Detail orientation

20. Determination
21. Drive
22. Emotional awareness
23. Empathy
24. Endurance
25. Explaining abilities
26. Follow-through
27. Forgiveness
28. Good judgement
29. Gratitude
30. Honesty
31. Hope
32. Humanity
33. Humility
34. Humour
35. Kindness
36. Leadership
37. Listening skills
38. Love
39. Love of learning
40. Moderation
41. Modesty
42. Moral compass
43. Optimism
44. Persistence
45. Personal responsibility
46. Perspective
47. Persuasion
48. Planning and organisational ability
49. Pride
50. Problem-solving skills
51. Prudence
52. Resilience
53. Self-awareness
54. Self-belief
55. Self-control
56. Self-expression
57. Sense of adventure
58. Sense of equality
59. Sense of fairness
60. Sense of innovation
61. Sense of service
62. Social connectivity
63. Social intelligence
64. Spirituality
65. Stickability
66. Storytelling ability
67. Strategic awareness
68. Teamwork ability
69. Time management
70. Vision
71. Wisdom
72. Work ethic
73. Zest for life

Acknowledgements

Prior to Violet's birth neither of us had been left unsupervised with a child. It seemed scandalous that two people who were so inexperienced and unqualified should be given the mammoth responsibility of raising a girl. It was other parents who offered us advice, support and kindness when we most needed it. While we consulted many experts from all different fields in writing this book, it was through listening to and watching other parents that we worked out the kind of parents we wanted to be. We hope that our book is giving back and paying it forward to our fellow parents.

Thank you to our formidable agents, Selwa Anthony and Linda Anthony, who have supported us and fought for us through the highs and the lows.

We are delighted and honoured to have published this book with Penguin Random House. Thank you to our publisher, Sophie Ambrose. From the very beginning, and every step of the way, we knew we were in the best of hands. Thank you to our editors, Fay Helfenbaum, Catherine Hill and Melissa Lane, and our proofreader, Beck Bauert, for your excellent advice. Thanks also to our publicist, Bella Arnott-Hoare, for your enthusiasm, strategy and insight.

We are extremely fortunate to have friends and family who not only support us, but care enough to be brutally honest. Thank you: Vanessa Alford, Sonja Ebbles, Jan Edwards, Kate Edwards, Michael Edwards, Kate Hall, Ellis James, Rebecca Lowth, Fiona McCahey, Carolyn Menzies, Alyson O'Shannessy, Jo Rosenberg, Frank Scanlon, Valerie Scanlon, Meg Sweeney, Wendy Tuohy and Louise White.

And to our darling Violet and Ivy: children often grow up striving to be good enough for their parents. We hope that in years to come you will look back on your childhoods and judge us to be good enough for you.

Notes

Introduction

1   'Students from 1600 cities just walked out of school to protest climate change. It could be Greta Thunberg's biggest strike yet', *Time*, 24 May 2019.

2   '10yo girl wins straw phase-out battle; Cairns Council agrees to ditch single-use plastics', ABC News, 11 April 2018.

3   Simmons, Rachel, *Enough As She Is: How to help girls move beyond impossible standards of success to live healthy, happy, and fulfilling lives*, HarperCollins, New York, 2018.

4   Lawrence, David, Sarah Johnson, Jennifer Hafekost, Katrina Boterhoven De Haan, Michael Sawyer, John Ainley, Stephen R. Zubrick, 'The mental health of children and adolescents: Report on the second Australian child and adolescent survey of mental health and wellbeing', Department of Health, Canberra, 2015.

5   Ibid.

6   'Women', Beyond Blue (accessed November 2019).

7   Australian Institute of Family Studies, 'The longitudinal study of Australian children annual statistical report 2016', AIFS, Melbourne, 2017.

8   Lawrence, David, Sarah Johnson, Jennifer Hafekost, Katrina Boterhoven De Haan, Michael Sawyer, John Ainley, Stephen R. Zubrick, 'The mental health of children and adolescents: Report on the second Australian child and adolescent survey of mental health and wellbeing', Department of Health, Canberra, 2015.

9   'Eating disorders prevention, treatment and management: An updated evidence review', The National Eating Disorders Collaboration, Crows Nest, 2017; nedc.com.au/research-and-resources/show/eating-disorders-prevention-treatment-and-management-an-updated-evidence-review (accessed 24 March 2020).

10 'Paying the price: The economic and social impact of eating disorders in Australia', The Butterfly Foundation, Crows Nest, 2012.

11 'Everyday sexism: Girls' and young women's views on gender inequality in Australia', Pan International and Our Watch survey, October 2016; apo.org.au/node/68539 (accessed 24 March 2020).

12 King, Madonna, *Fathers and Daughters: Helping girls and their dads build unbreakable bonds*, Hachette Australia, Sydney, 2018.

Chapter One

1 Strickland, Bonnie R., 'Internal versus external locus of control: An early history', *Perceived Control: Theory, research, and practice in the first 50 years*, John W. Reich and Frank J. Infurna (eds.), Oxford University Press, Oxford, 2016.

2 Seligman, Martin, *Flourish*, William Heinemann, Sydney, 2011.

3 Gale, Catharine R., G. David Batty, Ian J. Deary, 'Locus of control at age 10 years and health outcomes and behaviors at age 30 years: The 1970 British cohort study', *Psychosomatic Medicine*, vol. 70, no. 4, 2008, pp. 397–403.

4 Buchanan, Gregory McClellan, Martin Seligman, 'Explanatory style and heart disease', *Explanatory Style*, Gregory McClellan Buchanan and Martin Seligman (eds.), Erlbaum, Hillsdale, NJ, 1995, pp. 225–32.

5 Tindle, Hilary A. et al, 'Optimism, cynical hostility, and incident coronary heart disease and mortality in the Women's Health Initiative', *Circulation*, vol. 118, 2009, pp. 1145–6.

6 Cohen, Sheldon et al, 'Emotional style and susceptibility to the common cold', *Psychosomatic Medicine*, vol. 65, no. 4, 2003, pp. 652–7.

7 Doyle, William J. et al, 'Emotional style, nasal cytokines, and illness expression after experimental rhinovirus exposure', *Brain, Behaviour, and Immunity*, vol. 20, no. 2, 2006, pp. 175–81.

8 Seligman, *Flourish*.

9 Cloitre, Marylene, Richard G. Heimberg, Michael R. Liebowitz, Andrea Gitow, 'Perceptions of control in panic disorder and social phobia', *Cognitive Therapy and Research*, vol. 16, no. 5, 1992, pp. 569–77.

10 Burger, Jerry M., 'Desire for control, locus of control, and proneness to depression', *Journal of Personality*, vol. 52, no. 1, 1984, pp. 71–89.

11 Duckworth, Angela, *Grit: The power of passion and perseverance*, Random House UK, London, 2016.

12 Reivich, Karen, Andrew Shatté, *The Resilience Factor: 7 keys to finding your inner strength and overcoming life's hurdles*, Three Rivers, New York, 2003.

13 Seligman, *Flourish*.

14 Kelly, Rob, *Thrive*, Rob Kelly Publishing, Cambridge, 2012.

15 Seligman, Martin, with Karen Reivich, Lisa Jaycox and Jane Gillham, *The Optimistic Child*, Random House Australia, North Sydney, 2011.

Chapter Two

1 'Women's body talk: Perception stronger than reality?', ScienceDaily, November 2012 (accessed October 2019).

2 'Eating disorders prevention, treatment and management: An updated evidence review', The National Eating Disorders Collaboration, Crows Nest, 2017; nedc.com.au/research-and-resources/show/eating-disorders-prevention-treatment-and-management-an-updated-evidence-review (accessed 24 March 2020).

3 'Eating disorders – a current affair', The National Eating Disorders Collaboration, Crows Nest, 2012.

4 'What women are expected to spend on beauty amounts to a house deposit', *Sydney Morning Herald*, 11 June 2019.

5 Carlisle, Erin, Joann Fildes, Sabine Hall, Valancy Hicking, Brianna Perrens, Jacquelin Plummer, 'Youth survey report 2018', Mission Australia, Sydney, 2018.

6 Ibid.

7 'Girls aged five worry about their body image, say MPs', *Guardian*, 30 May 2012.

8 'Gere up for film', Page Six, 21 August 2012; pagesix.com/2012/08/21/gere-up-for-film/ (accessed 24 March 2020).

9 Tomiyama, A. Janet, Deborah Carr, Ellen M. Granberg, Brenda Major, Eric Robinson, Angelina R. Sutin, Alexandra Brewis, 'How and why weight stigma drives the obesity "epidemic" and harms health', *BMC Medicine*, vol. 16, no. 1, 2018.

10 'Weight management market by diet (meals, beverages, and supplements), by equipment (fitness and surgical), and by service (fitness centers, slimming centers, consultation services, and online weight loss services): Global industry perspective, comprehensive analysis, and forecast, 2018–2025', Zion Market Research, New York, 2019.

11 'The brain drain: Women would rather win "America's Next Top Model" than the Nobel Peace Prize', *The Independent*, 29 June 2011.

12 Engeln, Renee, *Beauty Sick: How the cultural obsession with appearance hurts girls and women*, HarperCollins, New York, 2018.

13 Mackintosh, Glenn, *Thinsanity: 7 steps to transform your mindset and say goodbye to dieting forever*, Hachette Australia, Sydney, 2019.

14 Bouchard, Claude, Angelo Tremblay, Jean-Pierre Després, André Nadeau, Paul J. Lupien, Germain Thériault, Jean Dussault, Sital Moorjani, Sylvie Pinault, Guy Fournier, 'The response to long-term overfeeding in identical twins', *New England Journal of Medicine*, vol. 322, no. 21, 1990.

15 Afzal, Shoaib, Anne Tybjærg-Hansen, Gorm B. Jensen, Børge G. Nordestgaard, 'Change in Body Mass Index associated with lowest mortality in Denmark, 1976–2013', *JAMA*, vol. 315, no. 18, 2016.

16 Fildes, Alison, Judith Charlton, Caroline Rudisill, Peter Littlejohns, A. Toby Prevost, Martin C. Gulliford, 'Probability of an obese person

attaining normal body weight: Cohort study using electronic health records', *American Journal of Public Health*, vol. 105, no. 9, 2015, pp. e54–9.

17 Mackintosh, *Thinsanity*.

18 '5 psychological tactics marketers use to influence consumer behavior', Fast Company, 7 June 2014.

19 'TV ads "have little effect" on children', *Guardian*, 11 November 2000.

20 'A look at Coca-Cola's advertising expenses', Investopedia, updated 21 September 2019.

21 'Eating tips for young toddlers', Better Health Channel, n.d.

Chapter Three

1 'Outcry as sex education chief warns forcing children to kiss relatives could be harmful', *Telegraph*, 8 Jan 2014.

2 'Hugs replaced with high fives in sexual consent course for kids', ABC News, 28 July 2019.

3 Thomas, Sara E., '"What should I do?": Young women's reported dilemmas with nude photographs', *Sexuality Research and Social Policy*, vol. 15, 2018, pp. 192–207.

4 Ibid.

5 'Reminder: She doesn't owe anyone a hug. Not even at the holidays', Girl Scouts of the USA, n.d.

6 TODAY Show, 'A PSA from Girls Scouts of America discourages parents from forcing their kids to hug relatives at the holidays. Do you agree with the Girl Scouts' stance on hugging?', Twitter, 22 November 2017; twitter.com/TODAYshow/status/933289666500894720 (accessed 24 March 2020).

7 'Why you should teach your kids correct names for genitals', *Globe and Mail*, 5 March 2015, updated 10 April 2018.

8 Elliot, Michele, Kevin Browne, Jennifer Kilcoyne, 'Child sexual abuse prevention: What offenders tell us', *Child Abuse & Neglect*, vol. 19, no. 5, 1995, pp. 579–94.

9 Simonis, Magdalena, Ramesh Manocha, Jason J. Ong, 'Female genital cosmetic surgery: A cross-sectional survey exploring knowledge, attitude and practice of general practitioners', *British Medical Journal*, vol. 6, no. 9, 2016.

10 Friday, Nancy, *My Mother/My Self: A daughter's search for identity*, Dell Publishing, New York, 1997.

Chapter Four

1 'Time to Live Report', IKEA Australia, 2013.

2 Shapiro, Jordan, *The New Childhood: Raising kids to thrive in a connected world*, Hachette Australia, Sydney, 2019.

3 Estroff Marano, Hara, *A Nation of Wimps: The high cost of invasive parenting*, Crown Archetype, New York, 2008.

4   Dent, Maggie, *Real Kids in an Unreal World*, Pennington Publications, Murwillumbah, 2016.

5   Witt, Sharon, *Raising Resilient Kids*, Collective Wisdom Publications, Mt Evelyn, 2018.

6   Waters, Lea, *The Strength Switch: How the new science of strength-based parenting can help your child and teen to flourish*, Ebury Australia, Sydney, 2017.

7   'High school students paying thousands to tutoring colleges in struggle for an academic edge', ABC News, 27 September 2017, updated 9 October 2017.

8   Carey, Tanith, *Taming the Tiger Parent: How to put your child's well-being first in a competitive world*, Robinson, London, 2014.

9   Ireson, Judith, Katie Rushforth, 'Private tutoring at transition points in the English education system: Its nature, extent and purpose', *Research Papers in Education*, vol. 26, no. 1, 2011, pp. 1–19.

10 Horsey, Mike, Richard Walker, *Reforming Homework: Practices, learning and policy*, Palgrave Macmillan, South Yarra, 2013, p. 10.

11 'Schooling & Homework', Maggie Dent, January 2020; maggiedent.com/common-concerns/schooling-homework (accessed 24 March 2020).

12 Horsey and Walker, *Reforming Homework*.

13 Kohn, Alfie, *The Homework Myth: Why our kids get too much of a bad thing*, Da Capo Press, New York, 2006.

14 Ibid.

15 'Reading for pleasure "boosts pupils' results in maths"', *Telegraph*, 11 September 2013.

16 Venning, Laura, 'Why is reading for pleasure important?', The Reading Agency, n.d. (accessed August 2019).

17 Kohn, Alfie, 'How to create non-readers: Reflections on motivation, learning, and sharing power', *English Journal*, vol. 100, no. 1, 2010, pp. 16–22.

18 'When novels were bad for you', *New York Times*, 14 September 2014.

19 'Does excessive screen time cause ADHD?', Psychology Today, 22 June 2019.

20 'American Academy of Pediatrics announces new recommendations for children's media use', American Academy of Pediatrics, 21 October, 2016; aap.org/en-us/about-the-aap/aap-press-room/Pages/American-Academy-of-Pediatrics-Announces-New-Recommendations-for-Childrens-Media-Use.aspx (accessed 24 March 2020).

21 See: 'Screen time and children', The Sydney Children's Hospitals Network, 9 August 2017, and 'Screen time and children: How to guide your child', Mayo Clinic, 20 June 2019.

22 'Guidelines on physical activity, sedentary behaviour and sleep for children under 5 years of age', World Health Organization; apps.who.int/iris/handle/10665/311664 (accessed 24 March 2020).

23   AAP Council on Communications and Media, 'Media and young minds', *Pediatrics*, vol. 138, no. 5, November 2016.

24   Nathanson, Amy I., Fashina Aladé, Molly L. Sharp, Eric E. Rasmussen, Katheryn Christy, 'The relation between television exposure and executive function among preschoolers', *Developmental Psychology*, vol. 50, no. 5, January 2014, p. 1501.

25   Ibid., p. 1503.

26   Bishop, Dorothy, 'An open letter to Baroness Susan Greenfield', BishopsBlog, 4 August 2011.

27   'Build screen time around family activities, not the other way round, parents told', Royal College of Paediatrics and Child Health, 4 January 2019.

28   esafety.gov.au

29   McKay, Sarah, *The Women's Brain Book*, Hachette Australia, Sydney, 2018.

Chapter Five

1   Seligman, Martin, with Karen Reivich, Lisa Jaycox and Jane Gillham, *The Optimistic Child*, Random House Australia, North Sydney, 2011.

2   Carey, Tanith, *Taming the Tiger Parent: How to put your child's well-being first in a competitive world*, Robinson, London, 2014.

3   Seligman, with Reivich, Jaycox and Gillham, *The Optimistic Child*.

4   Seligman, Martin, *Flourish*, William Heinemann, Sydney, 2011.

5   Witt, Sharon, *Raising Resilient Kids*, Collective Wisdom Publications, Mt Evelyn, 2018.

6   Robinson, Sir Ken, 'Do schools kill creativity?', TED, 2006; ted.com/talks/ken_robinson_says_schools_kill_creativity?language=en (accessed 24 March 2020).

7   Decety, Jean, Philip L. Jackson, Jessica A. Sommerville, Thierry Chaminade, Andrew N. Meltzoff, 'The neural bases of cooperation and competition: An fMRI investigation', *Neuroimage*, vol. 23, no. 2, 2004, pp. 744–51.

8   Carey, *Taming the Tiger Parent*.

9   Amabile, Teresa M., Beth Ann Hennessey, Barbara S. Grossman, 'Social influences on creativity: The effects of contracted-for reward', *Journal of Personality and Social Psychology*, vol. 50, no. 1, 1986, pp. 14–23.

10   Kohn, Alfie, *No Contest: The case against competition*, Mariner Books, Boston, 1993.

11   Henderlong, Jennifer, Mark R. Lepper, 'The effects of praise on children's intrinsic motivation: A review and synthesis', *Psychological Bulletin*, vol. 128, no. 5, 2002, pp. 774–95; pdfs.semanticscholar.org/8d0f/65c3b892fe622146 c42154b1b75943bf0688.pdf (accessed 24 March 2020).

Chapter Six

1   Seligman, Martin, with Karen Reivich, Lisa Jaycox and Jane Gillham, *The Optimistic Child*, Random House Australia, North Sydney, 2011.

2   Jones, Damon E., Mark Greenberg, Max Crowley, 'Early social-emotional functioning and public health: The relationship between kindergarten social competence and future wellness', *American Journal of Public Health*, vol. 105, no. 11, 2015, pp. 2283–90.

3   Teo, Alan R., HwaJung Choi, Marcia Valenstein, 'Social relationships and depression: Ten-year follow-up from a nationally representative study', *PLOS ONE*, vol. 8, no. 4, 2013; journals.plos.org/plosone/article?id= 10.1371/journal.pone.0062396 (accessed 24 March 2020).

4   'Loneliness is a social cancer, every bit as alarming as cancer itself', The Conversation, 19 November 2019.

5   'Helping children learn positive friendship skills', Kids Matter, 2011.

6   Mendler, Dr Allen, 'Teaching your students how to have a conversation', Edutopia, 5 November 2013.

7   Brown, Brené, *The Gifts of Imperfection: Let go of who you think you're supposed to be and embrace who you are*, Hazelden Publishing, Minnesota, 2010.

8   Monke, Audrey, '10 friendship skills every kid needs', Sunshine Parenting, n.d.; sunshine-parenting.com/wp-content/uploads/2018/12/10-Friendship-Skills-e-book-color.pdf (accessed 24 March 2020).

9   Whitson, Signe, *8 Keys to End Bullying: Strategies for parents & schools*, Norton Professional Books, New York, 2014.

10 Ibid.

11 King, Madonna, *Being 14: Helping fierce teens become awesome women*, Hachette Australia, Sydney, 2017.

12 'Aunties may be as important as mums when it comes to raising women', ABC Life, 20 September 2019.

13 Brickman, Philip, Dan Coates, Ronnie Janoff-Bulman, 'Lottery winners and accident victims: Is happiness relative?', *Journal of Personality and Social Psychology*, vol. 36, no. 8, 1978, pp. 917–27.

14 McKay, Sarah, *The Women's Brain Book*, Hachette Australia, Sydney, 2018.

15 Gable, Shelly L., Harry T. Reis, Emily A. Impett, Evan R. Asher, 'What do you do when things go right? The intrapersonal and interpersonal benefits of sharing positive events', *Journal of Personality and Social Psychology*, vol. 87, no. 2, 2004, pp. 228–45.

16 Cano, Tomás, Francisco Perales, Janeen Baxter, 'A Matter of Time: Father involvement and child cognitive outcomes', *Journal of Marriage and Family*, vol. 81, no. 1, 2019, pp. 164–84.

Chapter Seven

1   Benson, Peter L., *Sparks: How parents can ignite the hidden strengths of teenagers*, Jossey-Bass, San Francisco, 2008.
2   Simmons, Rachel, *The Curse of the Good Girl*, Penguin Books, New York, 2009.
3   'It has never been harder to bring up a daughter', *Telegraph*, 7 January 2013.
4   Siegel, Daniel J., Tina Payne Bryson, *The Whole-Brain Child*, Scribe Publications, Brunswick, 2012.
5   'Why Kristen Bell doesn't tell her kids "It's OK"', HuffPost, 10 May 2017.
6   'The dangers of the good child', *The Book of Life*, The School of Life, n.d. (accessed December 2019).
7   Polderman, Tinca C. et al, 'Meta-analysis of the heritability of human traits based on fifty years of twin studies', *Nature Genetics*, vol. 47, 2015, p. 702–9.
8   King, Madonna, *Fathers and Daughters: Helping girls and their dads build unbreakable bonds*, Hachette Australia, Sydney, 2018.

Appendix

1   strengthsprofile.com
2   Duckworth, Angela, *Grit: The power of passion and perseverance*, Random House UK, London, 2016.
3   'Find your 24 character strengths', VIA Institute, n.d.